Elementa Latina Or, Latin Lessons For Beginners

ELEMENTA LATINA

OR

LATIN LESSONS FOR BEGINNERS

BY

W. H. MORRIS

Author of 'Greek Lessons' &c.

. . ut pueris olim dant crustula blandi
Doctores, elementa velint ut discere prima
Hor. *Sat.* i. i.

THIRTY-THIRD IMPRESSION

WITH COMPLETE VOCABULARIES

√

LONGMANS, GREEN, AND CO.
39 PATERNOSTER ROW, LONDON
NEW YORK, BOMBAY, AND CALCUTTA

1914

PREFACE.

THESE Lessons are designed to carry beginners through the principal Inflexions of Latin words, and to teach them their use in the construction of easy sentences.

In the Accidence the principles of the "Public School Latin Primer" have generally been adopted, and the Stem-system has been gradually developed. In the Paradigms both the Latin Inflexions and their English Signs are printed in bolder type. By this means the learner will readily distinguish the Terminations from the Stem, and associate them in his mind with their English equivalents.

The construction of sentences is taught on a simple system of Analysis, supplemented by a few Syntactical rules. The sentences themselves have been drawn or adapted entirely from Caesar,*—the practice of selecting examples from authors of different periods and modes of expression tending rather to perplex the young student than to give him definite notions of the formation of a Latin sentence.

The book is divided into Sections (numbered 1, 2, etc.), each of which is subdivided into four Parts or Lessons.

Lesson A generally consists of a short portion of the Accidence to be committed to memory. It will be

---

* In which "is seen the unspotted propriety of the Latin tongue, even when it was at the highest pitch of all perfectness."—Ascham's 'Schoolmaster.'

found advantageous to repeat the Inflexions *without* as well as with the Stems.

Lesson B furnishes Grammar practice on the previous model, and cannot be too thoroughly learned.

Lesson C contains simple sentences, illustrating, *e.g.*, in the Nouns, the relation of the Subject to the Object, and familiarizing the learner with the use of the Nominative and Accusative Cases.

Lesson D shows how the simple form of sentence may be expanded by the addition of a Possessor, a Recipient, or an Instrument, exemplifying the use of the Genitive, Dative, and Ablative Cases.*

Irregular forms of Inflexion have been avoided until the Regular forms have been mastered.

The Quantities of the syllables have been marked where necessary, but the plan of reading over the lesson for the following day (if A or B) before dismissing the class, will often prevent faults in pronunciation which are afterwards difficult to eradicate.

A Parsing Scheme will be found at the end of the Lessons, which should be learned and practised *pari passu* with the successive steps of the student's progress.

The Author desires to acknowledge his obligations to E. Walford, Esq., M.A., for his valuable assistance in revising the work for the press.

---

* This part may be omitted, at the discretion of the teacher, until the learner has proceeded as far as the Recapitulatory Lesson

CONTENTS.

LATIN LESSONS.

---

1 (A). The Latin Alphabet has **25 Letters,** and is the same as the English without W.

The **Vowels** are **six—a, e, i, o, u, y.**

The other letters are **Consonants.**

Vowels marked thus (ˉ) are **long,** as ā in māte.

Those marked thus (ˇ) are **short,** as ă in măt.

The **Diphthongs** are **six,—**

Three in common use—**ae, oe,** and **au.**

Three rarely used—**ei, ui,** and **eu.**

(**ae** and **oe** are pronounced as long ē.)

The **Parts of Speech** in Latin are **eight.**

4 with Flexion (changes).	4 without Flexion.
Noun (Substantive).	Adverb.
Adjective.	Preposition.
Pronoun.	Conjunction.
Verb.	Interjection.

Note.—There is no Article in Latin : thus the Latin word **mensă** means **table, a table,** or **the table.**

B

DECLENSION OF NOUNS.

1 (B). Substantives are **declined** by Number and Case, Adjectives by Gender, Number, and Case.

The **Genders** are **three,**—

Masculine (*m.*), Feminine (*f.*), Neuter (*n.*).
Common Gender (*c.*) means either Masculine or Feminine.

The **Numbers** are **two,**--

Singular (*S.*), which speaks of **one.**
Plural (*P.*), which speaks of **more than one.**

> *Note.*—(*S.*) placed after a Noun shows that **it** has the Singular only, (*P.*) the Plural only.

The **Cases** are **six,**—

1. Nominative,   2. Vocative,   3. Accusative,
4. Genitive,   5. Dative,   6. Ablative.

1 (C). The **Nominative** names the **Subject,**—Who ? What ?—as,

The boy reads.—Who reads ?—The boy.
The fire burns.—What burns ?—The fire.
Then **boy** and **fire** are Nominatives.

The **Vocative** names the **Person** or **Thing addressed**— as,

O boy !　O fire !

The **Accusative** names the **Object,**—Whom ? What?— as,

The ball strikes the boy.—Strikes whom ?—The boy.
The child fears the fire.—Fears what ?—The fire.
Here **boy** and **fire** are Accusatives.

The **Genitive** names the **Author** or **Possessor**,—Of whom? Of what?—as,

> The book of the boy.—Of whom?—Of the boy.
> The heat of the fire.—Of what?—Of the fire.

Here **of the boy,** and **of the fire** are Genitives.

The **Dative** names the **Receiver** or **Indirect Object**,— To whom? To what? For whom? For what?—as,

> The master gives a book to the boy.—To whom? —To the boy.

Then **to the boy** is the Dative.

The **Ablative** names the **Instrument**,—With what?— as,

> The boy strikes the ball with the bat.—With what?—With the bat.

Then **with the bat** is the Ablative.

1 (D). Name the Cases of the Nouns in the following sentences, and give reasons for your answers :—

1. The sailor has a cottage.
2. The cottage of the sailor has a table.
3. Galba sees the gates of Rome.
4. Titus gives an arrow to the sailor.
5. The sailors of Galba wound the sailors of Titus with arrows.
6. The arrows of the sailors give victory to Titus.

2 (A).   First Declension (A-nouns).

The Nominative Singular generally ends in ă.

Gender—**Feminine**, except names of Males.

SINGULAR.

Nom., Mens-ă (*f.*)   a table.
Voc., Mens-ă   .   O table.
Acc., Mens-am .   a table.
Gen., Mens-ae .   of a table.
Dat., Mens-ae .   to or for a table.
Abl., Mens-ā   .   with, from, or by a table.

PLURAL.

Nom., Mens-ae   .   tables.
Voc., Mens-ae   .   O tables.
Acc., Mens-as   .   tables.
Gen., Mens-**Arum**   of tables.
Dat., Mens-īs .   .   to or for tables.
Abl., Mens-īs .   .   with, from, or by tables.

---

2 (B).   Learn and decline like Mensa :—

Căsa (*f.*), a cottage.
Porta (*f.*), a gate.
Pugna (*f.*), a battle.
Vīta (*f.*), life.
Rōma (*f.S.*), Rome.

Săgitta (*f.*), an arrow
Victorĭa (*f.*), victory.
Cōpĭae (*f.P.*), forces.
Nauta (*m.*), a sailor.
Galba (*m.S.*), Galba.

Rule 1.—The Verb agrees with its Nominative in Number and Person.

Rule 2.—Transitive Verbs govern an Accusative.

Note.—In translating a Latin sentence into English, take the Nominative **before** the Verb, the Accusative **after** it.

2 (C). **Verbs.**

Singular, 3rd Person.	Plural, 3rd Person.
hăbĕt, (he, she, it) has.	hăbent, (they) have.
dăt, (he, she, it) gives.	dant, (they) give.
vulnĕrăt, (he,she,it)wounds	vulnĕrant, (they) wound.

Translate into English :—
1. Nauta casam habet.
2. Casae mensas habent.
3. Galba sagittam dat.
4. Sagittae nautas vulnerant.
5. Pugnae victoriam dant.
6. Victoria vitam dat.

Translate into Latin :—
1. Rome has gates.
2. The cottage has a table.
3. The sailors wound Galba.
4. Galba has forces.
5. The sailor gives an arrow.
6. The arrows give victory.

2 (D). Translate into English :—
1. Casa nautae mensam habet.
2. Nautae sagittas Galbae habent.
3. Galba sagittas nautae dat.
4. Sagittae victoriam nautis dant.
5. Galba nautas sagittā vulnerat.
6. Nautae Galbam sagittis vulnerant.

Translate into Latin :—
1. The cottages of the sailors have tables.
2. Galba gives a cottage to the sailor.
3. Sailors have the cottages of Galba.
4. The victory of Galba gives life to the sailors.
5. The battles of the forces give victories to Galba.
6. The sailor wounds Galba with an arrow.

3 (A).   Second Declension (O-nouns).

Nouns in -us, -er, -ir, mostly Masculine, and in -um, Neuter.

(1). Masculine Nouns in -us.

SINGULAR

Nom.,	Dŏmĭn-ŭs (*m.*)	a lord.
Voc.,	Dŏmĭn-ĕ . .	O lord.
Acc.,	Dŏmĭn-um .	a lord.
Gen.,	Dŏmĭn-ī . .	of a lord.
Dat.,	Dŏmĭn-ō . .	to or for a lord.
Abl.,	Dŏmĭn-ō . .	with, from, or by a lord.

PLURAL.

Nom.,	Dŏmĭn-ī . .	lords.
Voc.,	Dŏmĭn-ī . .	O lords.
Acc.,	Dŏmĭn-ōs .	lords.
Gen.,	Dŏmĭn-Orum	of lords.
Dat.,	Dŏmĭn-īs . .	to or for lords.
Abl.,	Dŏmĭn-īs . .	with, from, or by lords.

---

3 (B). Learn and decline like Dominus :—

Servus (*m.*), a slave.	Vīcus (*m.*), a village.
Carrus (*m.*), a waggon.	Amīcus (*m.*), a friend.
Equus (*m.*), a horse.	Lēgātus (*m.*), a lieutenant.
Glădĭus (*m.*), a sword.	Gallus (*m.*), a Gaul.
Mūrus (*m.*), a wall.	Tītus (*m.S.*), Titus.

3 (C).   Verbs.

SINGULAR.	PLURAL.
vĭdĕt, (he, she, it) sees.	vĭdent, (they) see.
tĭmĕt, (he, she, it) fears.	tĭment, (they) fear.

1. Servus dominum timet.
2. Domini servos vident.
3. Carri equos habent.
4. Titus gladium dat.
5. Galli vicos habent.
6. Legatus muros videt.

1. The lord has a slave.
2. The slaves have swords.
3. The horses see the waggon.
4. Titus sees the Gauls.
5. The Gauls fear Titus
6. The lieutenant has a friend.

3 (D). 1. Servus equum domini habet.
2. Titus gladios Gallorum timet.
3. Legatus carros servis dat.
4. Galli vicos Tito dant.
5. Titus Gallum gladio vulnerat.
6. Servi amicos gladiis vulnerant.

1. The slaves have the horses of the lords.
2. The Gauls fear the sword of Titus.
3. The lieutenant gives a village to the friend.
4. The horses of Titus fear the walls.
5. The lords give waggons to the Gauls.
6. The Gauls wound the lieutenant with swords.

4 (A).   Second Declension (O-nouns).

(2). Masculine Nouns in -er, -ir.

SINGULAR.

Nom.,	Măgistĕr (*m.*) .	a master.
Voc.,	Măgistĕr . . .	O master.
Acc.,	Măgistr-um . .	a master.
Gen.,	Măgistr-ī . . .	of a master.
Dat.,	Măgistr-ō . .	to or for a master.
Abl.,	Măgistr-ō . .	with, from, or by a master.

PLURAL.

Nom.,	Măgistr-ī . . .	masters.
Voc.,	Măgistr-ī . . .	O masters.
Acc.,	Măgistr-ōs . .	masters.
Gen.,	Măgistr-Orum .	of masters.
Dat.,	Măgistr-īs . .	to or for masters.
Abl.,	Măgistr-īs . .	with, from, or by masters.

A few nouns in -er, -ir, retain the -er, -ir throughout.

SINGULAR.	PLURAL.
Nom., pŭĕr (*m.*), a boy.	*Nom.*, pŭĕr-ī.
Voc., pŭĕr.	*Voc.*, pŭĕr-ī.
Acc., pŭĕr-um.	*Acc.*, pŭĕr-ōs.
Gen., pŭĕr-ī.	*Gen.*, pŭĕr-Orum.
Dat., pŭĕr-ō.	*Dat.*, pŭĕr-īs.
Abl., pŭĕr-ō.	*Abl.*, pŭĕr-īs.

---

4 (B). Learn and decline

like Magister :—	like Puer :—
Ager (*m.*), a field.	**Sŏcer** (*m.*), a father-in-law.
Lĭber (*m.*), a book.	**Gĕner** (*m.*), a son-in-law.
Făber (*m.*), a workman.	**Signĭfer** (*m.*), a standard-
Arbĭter (*m.*), a judge.	**Vĭr** (*m.*), a man. [bearer.
Cimbri (*m.P.*), the Cimbri.	**Lĭbĕri** (*m.P.*), children.

4 (C).   Verbs

SINGULAR.	PLURAL.
ămăt, (he, she, it) loves.	ămant, (they) love.
dŏcĕt, (he, she, it) teaches.	dŏcent, (they) teach.

1. Magister pueros amat.
2. Puer librum habet.
3. Magistri libros dant.
4. Fabri liberos habent.
5. Arbiter agrum dat.
6. Soceri generos docent.

1. The masters teach the children.
2. The boys love the masters.
3. The son-in-law sees the father-in-law.
4. The standard-bearer fears the Cimbri.
5. The children love books.
6. The judges fear the men.

4 (D). 1. Liberi fabrorum libros amant.
2. Magister liberos signiferi docet.
3. Socer librum genero dat.
4. Cimbri agros signiferis dant.
5. Signifer puerum fabri vulnerat.
6. Arbitri agros viro dant.

1. The master teaches the children of the judge.
2. The masters give books to the children.
3. The children of the workman love the fields.
4. The judges teach the boys of the workmen.
5. The workman wounds the children of the Cimbri.
6. The judge has the fields of the son-in-law.

5 (A).   Second Declension (O-nouns).

(3). Neuter nouns in -um.

SINGULAR.

Nom.,	Bell-um (*n.*)	war.
Voc.,	Bell-um .	O war.
Acc.,	Bell-um .	war.
Gen.,	Bell-ī . .	of war.
Dat.,	Bell-ō . .	to or for war.
Abl.,	Bell-ŏ . .	with, from, or by war.

PLURAL.

Nom.,	Bell-ă . .	wars.
Voc.,	Bell-ă . .	O wars.
Acc.,	Bell-ă . .	wars.
Gen.,	Bell-Orum .	of wars.
Dat.,	Bell-īs . .	to or for wars.
Abl.,	Bell-īs . .	with, from, or by wars.

Note.—All Neuter nouns have the Nominative, Vocative, and Accusative alike in each Number, and in the Plural these always end in -a.

---

5 (B).   Learn and decline like Bellum :—

Rēgnum (*n.*), a kingdom.   Concĭlĭum (*n.*), a council.
Tēlum (*n.*), a dart, weapon.   Perīcŭlum (*n.*), danger.
Scūtum (*n*), a shield.   Cantĭum (*n.S.*), Kent.
Oppĭdum (*n.*), a town.   Castra (*n.P.*), a camp.
Praesĭdĭum (*n.*), a garrison,   Signum (*n.*), a standard, guard.   signal.

5 (C).   Verbs.

SINGULAR.	PLURAL.
āēfendĭt, (he, she, it) defends.	dēfendunt, (they) defend.
terrĕt, (he, she, it) frightens.	terrent, (they) frighten.

1. Regnum bella habet.
2. Bella pericula habent.
3. Praesidium castra defendit.
4. Tela praesidium terrent.
5. Oppida scuta habent.
6. Concilium periculum timet.

1. The kingdoms have garrisons.
2. Wars frighten the council.
3. The garrisons love wars.
4. The camp has dangers.
5. Kent has towns.
6. The garrison has standards.

---

5 (D). 1. Oppida Cantii praesidia habent.
2. Pericula castrorum praesidium terrent.
3. Concilium signa oppido dat.
4. Praesidium castra telis defendit.
5. Scuta praesidio dant.
6. Signa telis defendunt.

1. The dangers of war frighten the councils.
2. The council sees the danger of the towns.
3. The garrisons defend the towns with shields.
4. The council gives a standard to the garrison.
5. They wound the garrison with darts.
6. He defends the standard with a dart.

6 (A).   Third Declension (Consonant-nouns).

The Nominative Singular ends variously.

Consonant-nouns form the Genitive Plural in -um, preceded by a consonant.

Masculine and Feminine Nouns.

SINGULAR.

Nom.,	Consŭl (*m.*)	.	a consul.
Voc.,	Consŭl	. .	O consul.
Acc.,	Consŭl-em .	.	a consul.
Gen.,	Consŭl-ĭs .	.	of a consul.
Dat.,	Consŭl-ī .	.	to or for a consul.
Abl.,	Consŭl-ĕ .	.	with, from, or by a consul.

PLURAL.

Nom.,	Consŭl-ēs .	.	consuls.
Voc.,	Consŭl-ēs .	.	O consuls.
Acc.,	Consŭl-ēs .	.	consuls.
Gen.,	Consŭl-um	.	of consuls.
Dat.,	Consŭl-ĭbŭs	.	to or for consuls.
Abl.,	Consŭl-ĭbŭs	.	with, from, or by consuls.

---

6 (B). Learn and decline like Consul, taking care to form the Accusative, etc. from the Stem, which is givᴇn in the bracket:—

Caesar (Caesăr-)*m.S.*, Caesar
Sŏror (sorōr-) *f.*, a sister.
Frāter (fratr-) *m.*, a brother.
Lăpis (lapĭd-) *m.*, a stone.
Mīles (mīlĭt-) *m.*, a soldier.
Obses (obsĭd-) *c.*, a hostage.

Dux (dŭc-) *c.*, a leader.
Pax (pāc-) *f.S.*, peace.
Vox (vōc-) *f.*, a voice.
Sĕnŏnes *m.P.*, the Senones (a people of Gaul).

6 (C).   Verbs.

SINGULAR.	PLURAL.
occīdĭt, (he, she, it) kills.	occīdunt, (they) kill.
crēdit, (he, she, it) entrusts.	crēdunt, (they) entrust.

1. Duces milites habent.
2. Senones Caesarem timent.
3. Miles obsidem occidit.
4. Lapides consulem terrent.
5. Caesar pacem dat.
6. Frater sorores amat.

1. Caesar gives hostages.
2. The leader loves Caesar.
3. The Senones kill the soldiers.
4. The brothers defend the sister.
5. The soldier fears the stones.
6. The sister loves peace.

6 (D). 1. Milites Caesaris Senones terrent.
2. Dux Senonum obsides Caesari dat.
3. Consules obsidem lapidibus occidunt.
4. Caesar militem voce terret.
5. Consul milites Caesari credit.
6. Sorores lapides fratribus dant.

1. The soldier fears the voice of the leader.
2. The Senones give hostages to Caesar.
3. Caesar entrusts the hostages to the soldiers.
4. The leaders wound the hostages of the Senones with stones.
5. Caesar gives peace to the Senones.
6. The sisters of the soldiers love peace.

7 (A).   Third Declension. (I-nouns).

Masculine and Feminine Nouns in -is, -es, which do not increase in the Genitive Singular.

I-nouns form the Genitive Plural in -ium.

SINGULAR.

Nom.,	Ov-ĭs (*f.*) .	a sheep.
Voc.,	Ov-ĭs . .	0 sheep.
Acc.,	Ov-em . .	a sheep.
Gen.,	Ov-ĭs . .	of a sheep.
Dat.,	Ov-ī . . .	to or for a sheep.
Abl.,	Ov-ĕ . . .	with, from, or by a sheep.

PLURAL.

Nom.,	Ov-ēs . .	sheep.
Voc.,	Ov-ēs . .	0 sheep.
Acc.,	Ov-ēs or ĭs .	sheep.
Gen.,	Ov-Ium . .	of sheep.
Dat.,	Ov-ĭbŭs . .	to or for sheep.
Abl.,	Ov-ĭbŭs . .	with, from, or by sheep.

Many words with Stems ending in two Consonants belong to the I-nouns.

SINGULAR.	PLURAL.
Nom., Dens (*m.*), a tooth.	*Nom.*, Dent-ēs.
Voc., Dens.	*Voc.*, Dent-ēs
Acc., Dent-em.	*Acc.*, Dent-ēs or ĭs.
Gen., Dent-ĭs.	*Gen.*, Dent-Ium.
Dat., Dent-ī.	*Dat.*, Dent-ĭbŭs.
Abl., Dent-ĕ.	*Abl.*, Dent-ĭbŭs.

---

7 (B). Learn and decline like Ovis :—

Nāvis (*f.*), a ship.	**Fūnis** (*m.*), a rope.
Turris (*f.*), a tower	**Cīvis** (*c.*), a citizen.
Ignis (*m.*), a fire.	**Hostis** (*c.*), an enemy.

like Dens :—

Mons (mont-) *m.*, a mountain	**Urbs** (urb-) *f.*, the city.
Pons (pont-) *m.*, a bridge.	**Arx** (arc-) *f.*, a citadel.

7 (C).   Verbs.

SINGULAR.	PLURAL.
tĕnĕt, (he, she, it) holds.	**tĕnent**, (they) hold.
vastăt,(he,she,it)lays waste.	**vastant**, (they) lay waste.

1. Urbs arcem habet.
2. Hostes montem tenent.
3. Funis navem tenet.
4. Ignis urbem vastat.
5. Cives arcem tenent.
6. Turres pontem defendunt.

1. Fire lays waste the cities.
2. The enemy holds the citadel.
3. The citizens hold the bridge.
4. The tower defends the city.
5. The ropes hold the ships.
6. The enemy kills the citizens.

7 (D). 1. Cives pontem urbis tenent.
2. Ignis urbes hostium vastat.
3. Cives arcem hostibus dant.
4. Hostes urbem igne vastant.
5. Civis navem fune tenet.
6. Montem turribus defendunt.

1. The ships of the citizens frighten the enemy.
2. The citizens defend the bridge with ships.
3. The enemy lays waste the citadel with fire.
4. The citizen gives the towers to the enemy.
5. They hold the ships with ropes.
6. The towers of the enemy frighten the citizens.

8 (A). Third Declension—Neuter Nouns
Consonant-nouns.

SINGULAR.

Nom.,	Nōmĕn (*n.*) . . .	a name.
Voc.,	Nōmĕn . . .	O name.
Acc.,	Nōmĕn . . .	a name.
Gen.,	Nōmĭn-ĭs . . .	of a name.
Dat.,	Nōmĭn-ī . . .	to or for a name.
Abl.,	Nōmĭn-ĕ . . .	with, from, or by a name.

PLURAL.

Nom.,	Nōmĭn-ă . . .	names.
Voc.,	Nōmĭn-ă . . .	O names.
Acc.,	Nōmĭn-ă . . .	names.
Gen.,	Nōmĭn-um : .	of names.
Dat.,	Nōmĭn-ĭbŭs . .	to or for names.
Abl.,	Nōmĭn-ĭbŭs . .	with, from, or by names.

I-nouns (in e, al, ar).

SINGULAR.	PLURAL.
Nom., Mărĕ (*n.*), a sea.	*Nom.,* Măr-ĭă
Voc., Mărĕ.	*Voc.,* Măr-ĭă.
Acc., Mărĕ.	*Acc.,* Măr-ĭă.
Gen., Măr-ĭs.	*Gen.,* Măr-Ium.
Dat., Măr-ī.	*Dat.,* Măr-ĭbŭs.
Abl., Măr-ī.	*Abl.,* Măr-ĭbŭs.

---

8 (B). Learn and decline like Nomen :—

Agmĕn (agmĭn-), *n.*, an army (on march).

Flūmĕn(flūmĭn-), *n.*, a river.

Căpŭt (căpĭt-), *n.*, a head, source.

Onus (ŏnĕr-), *n.*, a burden.

Corpus (corpŏr-), *n.*, a body.

Vulnus (vulnĕr-), *n.*, a wound.

Iter (ĭtĭnĕr-), *n.*, a journey, march, road.

like Mare :—

Rēte (rēt-), *n.*, a net.
Ănĭmăl (ănĭmāl-), *n.*, an animal.
Moenĭă, *n.P.*, ramparts.

8 (C).   **Verbs.**

SINGULAR.	PLURAL.
impĕdĭt, (he, she, it) hinders	**impĕdĭunt**, (they) hinder.
făcĭt, (he, she, it) makes.	**făcĭunt**, (they) make.

1. Agmen iter facit.
2. Corpus vulnera habet.
3. Onus animal impedit.
4. Flumina nomina habent.
5. Moenia agmen terrent.
6. Animalia capita habent.

1. The journey frightens the army (on march).
2. The army sees the ramparts.
3. Wounds hinder the animals.
4. The armies make journeys.
5. The head has a wound.
6. The sea has nets.

---

8 (D). 1. Itinera agminis animalia terrent.
2. Mare iter agminis impedit.
3. Onera animalium iter impediunt.
4. Agmen vulnera animalibus dat.
5. Caput animalis vulnus habet.
6. Agmina oneribus impediunt.

1. The army sees the source of the river.
2. Rivers hinder the march of the army.
3. They give names to the rivers.
4. He hinders the animal with a burden.
5. He gives wounds to the animal.
6. The army frightens the animals with wounds.

C

9 (A).   Fourth Declension (U-nouns).

Nouns ending in -us and -u.

Masculine and Feminine Nouns in -us.

SINGULAR.

Nom.,	Grăd-ŭs (*m.*) .	a step.
Voc.,	Grăd-ŭs . . .	O step.
Acc.,	Grăd-um . .	a step.
Gen.,	Grăd-ūs . . .	of a step.
Dat.,	Grăd-ŭī . . .	to or for a step.
Abl.,	Grăd-ū . . .	with, from, or by a step.

PLURAL.

Nom.,	Grăd-ūs . . .	steps.
Voc.,	Grăd-ūs . . .	O steps.
Acc.,	Grăd-ūs . . .	steps.
Gen.,	Grăd-Uum . .	of steps.
Dat.,	Grăd-ĭbŭs . .	to or for steps.
Abl.,	Grăd-ĭbŭs, . .	with, from, or by steps.

Neuter Nouns in -u.

Nom.,	Gĕn-ū (*n.*), a knee.	*Nom.*,	Gĕn-ŭă.
Voc.,	Gĕn-ū.	*Voc.*,	Gĕn-ŭă.
Acc.,	Gĕn-ū.	*Acc.*,	Gĕn-ŭă.
Gen.,	Gĕn-ūs.	*Gen.*,	Gĕn-Uum.
Dat.,	Gĕn-ū.	*Dat.*,	Gĕn-ĭbŭs.
Abl.,	Gĕn-ū.	*Abl.*,	Gĕn-ĭbŭs.

A few have -ubus in the Dative and Ablative Plural.

---

9 (B). Learn and decline like Gradus :—

Currus (*m.*), a chariot.	**Impĕtus** (*m.*), an attack.
Ictus (*m.*), a blow.	**Exercĭtus** (*m.*), an army.
Portus (*m.*), a harbour.	**Manus** (*f.*), the hand.
Adventus (*m.S.*), an approach.	**Equĭtātus** (*m.S.*), cavalry.
	Sĕnātus (*m.S.*), the Senate.

like Genu :—
Cornu (*n.*), a horn, wing of an army.

---

9 (C). **Verbs.**

SINGULAR. | PLURAL.
frangit, (he, she, it) breaks. | **frangunt,** (they) break.
laudăt, (he, she, it) praises. | **laudant,** (they) praise.

---

1. Exercitus impetum facit.
2. Currūs equitatum terrent.
3. Senatus exercitum laudat.
4. Manus ictum dat.
5. Equitatus portum defendit.
6. Cornua currūs frangunt.

1. The chariots make an attack.
2. The cavalry break the chariots.
3. Blows frighten the senate.
4. The armies defend the harbours.
5. The senate praises the cavalry.
6. The wing (of the army) has chariots.

---

9 (D). 1. Senatus adventum curruum videt.
2. Ictūs equitatūs currum frangunt.
3. Exercitus senatum ictibus vulnerat.
4. Impetus equitatūs exercitum terret.
5. Cornua exercitūs equitatum timent.
6. Senatus portum exercitui credit.

1. The approach of the army frightens the senate.
2. The senate praises the attack of the cavalry.
3. The wing of the army makes an attack.
4. Chariots hinder the attack of the wing.
5. The cavalry give blows to the senate.
6. The senate defends the harbours with chariots.

10 (A).   Fifth Declension (E-nouns).

Nouns ending in -ēs.

Feminine, except Diĕs, which is sometimes Masculine in the Singular, and always Masculine in the Plural; and Meridiēs, which is Masculine.

SINGULAR.

Nom.,	Dĭ-ēs	. .	a day.
Voc.,	Dĭ-ēs	. .	O day.
Acc.,	Dĭ-em	. .	a day.
Gen.,	Dĭ-ēī	. .	of a day.
Dat.,	Dĭ-ēī	. .	to or for a day.
Abl.,	Dĭ-ē	. .	with, from, or by a day.

PLURAL.

Nom.,	Dĭ-ēs	. .	days.
Voc.,	Dĭ-ēs	. .	O days.
Acc.,	Dĭ-ēs	. .	days.
Gen.,	Dĭ-Erum	.	of days.
Dat.,	Dĭ-ēbŭs	.	to or for days.
Abl.,	Dĭ-ēbŭs	.	with, from, or by days.

---

10 (B). Learn and decline like Dies :—

Rēs (*f.*), a thing, affair.
Fĭdes (*f.S.*), faith.
Plānĭtĭes (*f.S.*), a plain.
Pernĭcĭes (*f.S.*), destruction
Mĕrīdĭes (*m.S.*), noon.
Spēs (*f.*), hope.
Spĕcĭes (*f.*), an appearance.
Plēbes (*f.S.*), the common people.
Acĭes (*f.*), an army (in line of battle).

Note.—Spes, Species and Acies have no Genitive, Dative, or Ablative Plural. A Consonant before ei shortens the ĕ, as Rĕi.

10 (C).   Verb.

SINGULAR.	PLURAL.
vincĭt, (he, she, it) conquers.	**vincunt,** (they) conquer.

---

1. Acies planitiem defendit.
2. Pernicies plebem terret.
3. Res aciem impediunt.
4. Dies spem dat.
5. Plebes fidem habet.
6. Species spes dat.

1. The army fears destruction.
2. The appearance frightens the people
3. The affair gives hope.
4. They defend the faith.
5. The armies hold the plain.
6. Destruction frightens the army.

---

10 (D). 1. Pernicies aciei plebem terret.
2. Res spem aciei dant.
3. Acies perniciem rerum timet.
4. Species perniciei aciem terret.
5. Spes vincit.
6. Aciem pernicie terrent.

1. The appearance of the plain frightens the people.
2. The people entrust the affairs to the army.
3. Noon gives hope to the people.
4. By faith they conquer.
5. Under (with) the appearance of faith the army holds the plain.
6. The people see the destruction of the army.

11 (A).   The Five Declensions of Nouns.

1. To what Declension do A-nouns belong? E-nouns? I-nouns? O-nouns? U-nouns? Consonant-nouns?

2. What is the Ending of the Nominative Singular of the First Declension? Of the Second Declension? Of the Third Declension? Of the Fourth Declension? Of the Fifth Declension?

3. What is the Gender of the First Declension? Of the Second? Of the Third? Of the Fourth? Of the Fifth?

4. Repeat all the Declensions of Nouns (A 2—10).

---

11 (B). The Declension to which a Noun belongs is known by the Ending of its Genitive case.

The letter which precedes -**rum** or -**um** in the Genitive Plural is called the **Character** of the Declension.

		GEN. SING.			GEN. PLUR.
First Declension	.	-ae	.	.	-**Arum.**
Second ,,	.	-ī	.	.	-**Orum.**
Third ,,	.	-īs	.	.	-**um*** or **Ium.**
Fourth ,,	.	-ūs	.	.	-**Uum.**
Fifth ,,	.	-ēī	.	.	-**Erum.**

Repeat and decline all the Nouns in the Vocabularies (B 2—10), giving the Genders, and saying to which Declension each Noun belongs.

* Preceded by a Consonant.

11 (C). 1. Roma muros habet. *
2. Galli sagittas tenent.
3. Caesar impetum facit.
4. Lapides equos terrent.
5. Sorores spem habent.
6. Onera servos impediunt.

1. The Gauls have chariots.
2. Shields defend the soldiers.
3. Mountains hinder the army (on march).
4. The cavalry lays waste the plain.
5. Ships defend the harbour.
6. Cities have gates.

---

11 (D). 1. Copiae Caesaris Gallos vincunt.
2. Titus civem gladio occidit.
3. Dux castra praesidio defendit.
4. Victoria spem exercitui dat.
5. Hostes arcem igne vastant.
6. Miles telum manu frangit.

1. Caesar sees the walls of Rome.
2. Rivers hinder the approach of the Cimbri.
3. Titus gives darts to the citizens.
4. The sailors defend the harbour with ships.
5. The Senones wound the garrison with arrows.
6. The leaders of the Gauls give peace to the city

* Parse all the Latin nouns on this page. (See page 111)

ADJECTIVES.

12 (A). Adjectives of the 1st and 2nd Declensions in -us, -a, -um.

Bŏnŭs (*m.*), bŏnă (*f.*), bŏnum (*n.*), good.
The Masculine is declined like Dominus.
The Feminine   „   like Mensa.
The Neuter   „   like Bellum.

SINGULAR.

	Masc.	*Fem.*	*Neut.*
Nom.,	Bŏn-ŭs	bŏn-ă	bŏn-um.
Voc.,	Bŏn-ĕ	bŏn-ă	bŏn-um.
Acc.,	Bŏn-um	bŏn-am	bŏn-um.
Gen.,	Bŏn-ī	bŏn-ae	bŏn-ī.
Dat.,	Bŏn-ō	bŏn-ae	bŏn-ō.
Abl.,	Bŏn-ō	bŏn-ā	bŏn-ō.

PLURAL.

Nom.,	Bŏn-ī	bŏn-ae	bŏn-ă.
Voc.,	Bŏn-ī	bŏn-ae	bŏn-ă.
Acc.,	Bŏn-ōs	bŏn-ās	bŏn-ă.
Gen.,	Bŏn-ōrum	bŏn-ārum	bŏn-ōrum.
Dat.,	Bŏn-īs	bŏn-īs	bŏn-īs.
Abl.,	Bŏn-īs	bŏn-īs	bŏn-īs.

12 (B). Learn and decline like Bonus :—

măl-us, a, um, bad.	tĭmĭd-us, a, um, timid.
magn-us, a, um, great.	alt-us, a, um, high, deep.
parv-us, a, um, little, small.	firm-us, a, um, firm, strong.
clar-us, a, um, famous.	long-us, a, um, long.
dūr-us, a, um, hard, cruel.	lăt-us, a, um, broad.

Decline together :—

1. Bonus dominus.   4. Clarus consul.
2. Parva mensa.   5. Altum mare.
   . Durum bellum   6. Magna res.

12 (C). *Rule* 3.—Adjectives agree with their Substantives in Gender, Number, and Case.

Note.—In Latin the Adjective is often placed **after** its Substantive.

1. Bonus dominus timidum servum habet.
2. Pugna longa victoriam magnam dat.
3. Alti muri milites duros terrent.
4. Acies magnae firmas arces defendunt.
5. Clari duces oppida parva terrent.
6. Exercitus magni latos agros vastant.

1. Bad masters have timid slaves.
2. The famous leader defends the strong city.
3. The broad river hinders great armies.
4. The long arrows wound the cruel enemy.
5. A small rope holds the great ship.
6. The deep sea frightens timid sailors.

---

12 (D). 1. Titus equum duri militis videt.
2. Frater bonus librum parvo puero dat.
3. Caesar nautam longā sagittā occidit.
4. Cives timidi tela hostium durorum timent.
5. Cimbri oppidum magnum altis moenibus defendunt.
6. Adventus agminis spem magnam civibus timidis dat.

1. The timid sheep love the high mountains.
2. The brother gives an arrow to the little sister.
3. The Gauls see the ramparts of the great city.
4. Titus kills the bad sailor with hard blows.
5. The soldiers of Caesar defend the high towers with great stones.
6. They entrust great armies to the famous leader.

13 (A). Adjectives of the 1st and 2nd Declensions in -er, -a, -um.

The Masculine is declined like Magister or Puer.

(1) **Nĭgĕr** (*m.*), **nigră** (*f.*), **nigrum** (*n.*), black.

SINGULAR.

	Masc.	*Fem.*	*Neut.*
Nom.,	Nĭgĕr	nigr-ă	nigr-um
Voc.,	Nĭgĕr	nigr-ă	nigr-um
Acc.,	Nigr-um	nigr-am	nigr-um
Gen.,	Nigr-ī	nigr-ae	nigr-ī
Dat.,	Nigr-ŏ	nigr-ae	nigr-ŏ
Abl.,	Nigr-ŏ	nigr-ā	nigr-ō

PLURAL.

	Masc.	*Fem.*	*Neut.*
Nom.,	Nigr-ī	nigr-ae	nigr-ă
Voc.,	Nigr-ī	nigr-ae	nigr-ă
Acc.,	Nigr-ŏs	nigr-ās	nigr-ă
Gen.,	Nigr-ōrum	nigr-ārum	nigr-ōrum
Dat.,	Nigr-īs	nigr-īs	nigr-īs
Abl.,	Nigr-īs	nigr-īs	nigr-īs

(2) **Tĕnĕr, tĕnĕră, tĕnĕrum,** tender.

	SINGULAR.			PLURAL.		
	Masc.	*Fem.*	*Neut.*	*Masc.*	*Fem.*	*Neut.*
Nom.,	Tĕnĕr	-ă	-um	Tĕnĕr-ī	-ae	-ă
Voc.,	Tĕnĕr	-ă	-um	Tĕnĕr-ī	-ae	-ă
Acc.,	Tĕnĕr-um	-am	-um	Tĕnĕr-ŏs	-ās	-ă
Gen.,	Tĕnĕr-ī	-ae	-ī	Tĕnĕr-ōrum	-ārum	-ōrum
Dat.,	Tĕnĕr-ŏ	-ae	-ō	Tĕnĕr-īs	-īs	-īs
Abl.,	Tĕnĕr-ŏ	-ā	-ō	Tĕnĕr-īs	-īs	-īs

---

13 (B). Learn and decline like Niger :—

Pulcher, beautiful, fair.	**Aeger,** sick.
Săcer, sacred.	**Noster,** our, ours.
Crēber, frequent.	**Vester,** your, yours.

like Tener :—

| Miser, wretched. | Liber, free. |
| Asper, rough, fierce. | Dext -er, -era, -erum, or -ra, -rum, right. |

Decline together :—
1. Niger equus.
2. Pulchra manus.
3. Sacrum flumen.
4. Mons asper.
5. Tenera soror.
6. Miserum bellum.

---

13 (C). 1. Tener puer servum nigrum timet.
2. Hostes crebri miseras sorores occidunt.
3. Aspera pugna vulnera misera dat.
4. Crebri ictus milites aegros terrent.
5. Liberi cives arcem sacram defendunt.
6. Corpora aegra viros nostros impediunt.

1. The tender sister loves the sacred river.
2. Our leaders kill the wretched hostages.
3. Your enemies hold the sacred citadel.
4. The right wing makes frequent attacks.
5. Fierce wars frighten our army.
6. Beautiful ships defend our harbours.

---

13 (D). 1. Galba turres arcis sacrae videt.
2. Adventus navium nostrarum nigros nautas terret.
3. Militem aegrum crebris ictibus vulnerant.
4. Titus currum sorori pulchrae dat.
5. Gladium dextrā manu tenet.
6. Legatus oppidum civibus liberis dat.

1. The friends of the sick soldier love peace.
2. Our sailors wound the Cimbri with frequent arrows.
3. They see the destruction of the wretched citizens.
4. Caesar gives peace to the sick soldiers.
5. The sailor sees the source of the sacred river.
6. Our (men) lay waste the fair cities with fire.

14 (A).   Adjectives of the Third Declension.

(1) Two Endings in the Nominative Singular.

Mĕliŏr (*m.* and *f.*), **mĕliŭs** (*n.*), better.

	SINGULAR.			PLURAL.	
	M. and *F.*	*N.*		*M.* and *F.*	*N.*
Nom.,	Mĕliŏr	mĕliŭs	*Nom.*,	Mĕliŏr-ēs	mĕliŏr-ă
Voc.,	Mĕliŏr	mĕliŭs	*Voc.*,	Mĕliŏr-ēs	mĕliŏr-ă
Acc.,	Mĕliŏr-em	mĕliŭs	*Acc.*,	Mĕliŏr-ēs	mĕliŏr-ă
Gen.,	Mĕliŏr-ĭs		*Gen.*,	Mĕliŏr-um	
Dat.,	Mĕliŏr-ī		*Dat.*,	Mĕliŏr-ĭbŭs	
Abl.,	Mĕliŏr-ĕ or ī		*Abl.*,	Mĕliŏr-ĭbŭs	

Tristĭs (*m.* and *f.*), **tristĕ** (*n.*), sad.

	SINGULAR.			PLURAL.	
	M. and *F.*	*N.*		*M.* and *F.*	*N.*
Nom.,	Trist-ĭs	trist-ĕ	*Nom.*,	Trist-ēs	trist-ĭă
Voc.,	Trist-ĭs	trist-ĕ	*Voc.*,	Trist-ēs	trist-ĭă
Acc.,	Trist-em	trist-ĕ	*Acc.*,	Trist-ēs	trist-ĭă
Gen.,	Trist-ĭs		*Gen.*,	Trist-ĭum	
Dat.,	Trist-ī		*Dat.*,	Trist-ĭbŭs	
Abl.,	Trist-ī		*Abl.*,	Trist-ĭbŭs	

A few have Three Endings in the Nom. and Voc. Sing.—as,

Nom. Voc.,   **Acĕr** (*m.*), **ācris** (*f.*), **ācrĕ** (*n.*), sharp, eager.

Acc.,   **Acr-em** (*m. & f.*), **ācr-ĕ** (*n.*), etc., like Tristis.

14 (B). Learn and decline like Melior :—

Grăviŏr, heavier. | **Fortiŏr,** stronger.

like Tristis :—

Brĕv-is, e, short. | **Fort-is, e,** strong, brave.
Grăv-is, e, heavy. | **Fĭdēl-is, e,** faithful.
Lĕv-is, e, light. | **Crūdēl-is, e,** cruel.
Omn-is, e, every, all. | **Cĕlĕr, cĕlĕr-is, e,** swift, quick (as acer).

Decline together :—

1. Melior puer.   3. Vir fortis.   5. Celeris sagitta.
2. Gravius onus. 4. Triste nomen. 6. Acre bellum.

---

14 (C). 1. Fortis miles telum breve habet.
2. Bellum crudele tristes cives terret.
3. Celeres sagittae servum fidelem occidunt.
4. Gravia onera servos fortiores impediunt.
5. Omnes milites celeres equos habent.
6. Soror fratrem fortem amat.

1. The sailor has faithful friends.
2. The heavy burden hinders the swift horse.
3. The animals have stronger bodies.
4. Caesar praises all the army.
5. A short battle gives swift victory.
6. The light arrows give heavier wounds.

---

14 (D). 1. Titus amicum vulnere crudeli occidit.
2. Consul corpus viri fortis videt.
3. Faber tela servo fideli dat.
4. Legatus hostem levi sagitta vulnerat.
5. Adventus curruum gravium Gallos terret.
6. Nautae portum navibus celeribus defendunt.

1. The walls of strong towns have towers.
2. Titus kills the sad hostage with a short sword.
3. The master gives books to all the boys.
4. The workman breaks the light weapon with a strong hand.
5. The boy loves the voice of the faithful friend.
6. The father-in-law gives a swift horse to the brave son-in-law

15 (A).   Adjectives of the Third Declension.

(2) One Ending in the Nominative Singular.

Ingens (*m.*, *f.*, and *n.*), immense.

	SINGULAR.			PLURAL.	
	M. and *F.*	*N.*		*M.* and *F.*	*N.*
Nom.,	Ingens		*Nom.*,	Ingent-ēs	ingent-ĭă
Voc.,	Ingens		*Voc.*,	Ingent-ēs	ingent-ĭă
Acc.,	Ingent-em	ingens	*Acc.*,	Ingent-ēs	ingent-ĭă
Gen.,	Ingent-ĭs		*Gen.*,	Ingent-ĭum	
Dat.,	Ingent-ĭ		*Dat.*,	Ingent-ĭbŭs	
Abl.,	Ingent-ī or ĕ		*Abl.*,	Ingent-ĭbŭs	

Fēlix (*m.*, *f.*, and *n.*), happy.

	SINGULAR.			PLURAL.	
	M. and *F.*	*N.*		*M.* and *F.*	*N.*
Nom.,	Fēlix		*Nom.*,	Fēlīc-ēs	fēlīc-ĭă
Voc.,	Fēlix		*Voc.*,	Fēlīc-ēs	fēlīc-ĭă
Acc.,	Fēlīc-em	fēlix	*Acc.*,	Fēlīc-ēs	fēlīc-ĭă
Gen.,	Fēlīc-ĭs		*Gen.*,	Fēlīc-ĭum	
Dat.,	Fēlīc-ī		*Dat.*	Fēlīc-ĭbŭs	
Abl.,	Fēlīc-ī or ĕ		*Abl.*,	Fēlīc-ĭbŭs	

---

15 (B). Learn and decline like Ingens :—

Prūdens (prūdent-),prudent
Pŏtens (pŏtent-), powerful.
Innŏcens (innŏcent-), inno-cent.

Rĕcens (rĕcent-), recent.
Absens (absent-), absent.
Pătĭens (patient-),patient.

like Felix :—

Fĕrox (fĕrōc-), fierce.
Vēlox (vēlōc-), swift.

Fĕrax (fĕrāc-), fruitful.
Duplex (duplĭc-), double.

Decline together :—

1. Potens dominus.
2. Soror patiens.
3. Ferax ager.
4. Duplex acies.
5. Animal patiens.
6. Ferox agmen.

15 (C). 1. Magister patientem puerum amat.
  2. Soror animalia ferocia timet.
  3. Caesar duces prudentes laudat.
  4. Recens vulnus militem ferocem impedit.
  5. Hostes agros feraces vastant.
  6. Dux aciem duplicem habet.

  1. The fierce soldier kills the innocent hostage.
  2. Swift animals frighten the boys.
  3. The lord praises the patient slaves.
  4. Titus teaches the happy boy.
  5. The Cimbri have swift horses.
  6. The powerful leader has immense forces.

---

15 (D). 1. Flumina adventum agminis ingentis impediunt.
  2. Soror puerorum felicium pericula timet.
  3. Consul absens exercitum duci prudenti credit.
  4. Caesar Gallum ingenti vulnere occidit.
  5. Tela Galli ferocis consulem terrent.
  6. Equitatus planitiem feracem equis velocibus vastat.

  1. The army of the absent leader makes an attack.
  2. Mountains hinder the marches of immense armies.
  3. The horns of the fierce animals give wounds.
  4. Caesar makes an attack with swift ships.
  5. The lord frightens the patient slave with an immense burden.
  6. Galba defends the city with a double line-of-battle

ADJECTIVES.

16 (A). All the Adjectives.

1. In what do Adjectives agree with their Substantives?

2. To what Declensions do Adjectives in -us, -a, -um, and -er, -a, -um, belong?

3. To which Declension do all other Adjectives belong?

4. How many Endings in the Nom. Sing. have Adjectives of the Third Declension?

5. Which take -um, and which -ium, in the Genitive Plural?

6. Which have -i in the Ablative Singular? Which have -e?

7. Repeat all the Declensions of Adjectives (A 12—15).

16 (B).

1. Repeat and decline all the Adjectives in the Vocabularies (B 12—15), saying which Declensions they are like.

2. Decline together all the Nouns and Adjectives given in B 12—15.

16 (C). 1. Nauta bonus pulchram urbem defendit.
2. Feroces milites arcem firmam tenent.
3. Animalia velocia ictus duros timent.
4. Domini potentes fidelem servum laudant.
5. Celeris sagitta vulnus asperum dat.
6. Flumina lata exercitus magnos impediunt.

1. Sharp war frightens the timid sailor.
2. The cruel Gauls lay waste the fruitful fields.
3. The beautiful sisters praise the long peace
4. The happy boys fear the frequent stones.
5. The broad sea has immense harbours.
6. Our enemies have stronger bodies.

---

16 (D). 1. Titus obsidem aegrum brevi telo vulnerat.
2. Nostri milites castra scutis parvis defendunt.
3. Dux victorias recentes exercituum vestrorum laudat.
4. Corpora animalium omnium capita habent.
5. Servus equo patienti gravius vulnus dat.
6. Faber gladium levem ictu gravi frangit.

1. The fierce Cimbri break the gates of the high citadel.
2. The son-in-law of the good sailor has long nets.
3. The little boy fears the horns of the fierce animals.
4. The sailors hold the swift ships with a long rope.
5. Caesar lays waste strong towns of Kent with cruel war.
6. The approach of the swift cavalry gives great hope to the wretched citizen.

D

17 (A). The **Degrees of Comparison** are **three,—**
Positive, Comparative, and Superlative.

Positive.	Comparative.	Superlative.
as Dūrŭs	dūrĭŏr	dūrissĭmŭs
hard	*harder*	*hardest,* or *very hard*
Clārŭs	clārĭŏr	clārissĭmŭs
famous	*more famous*	*most,* or *very famous*

The Comparative is formed by adding **-ĭŏr,** and the Superlative by adding **-issĭmŭs** to the Stem.

Note.—To find the Stem of a Noun or Adjective, take away the ending of the Genitive,—as

from **Dūrŭs**—*Genitive* dūr-ī, *Stem* **dūr-,** are formed
Comp. dūr-ĭŏr, *Sup.* dūr-issĭmŭs.

from **Fēlix**—*Genitive* fēlīc-ĭs, *Stem* **fēlīc-,** are formed
Comp. fēlīc-ĭŏr, *Sup.* fēlīc-issĭmŭs.

Adjectives in **-ĕr** form the Superlative by adding **-rĭmus** to the Positive,—as

Pos. Nĭgĕr, *Comp.* nigr-ĭŏr, *Sup.* nĭger-rĭmŭs

---

17 (B). Comparatives are declined like Melior.
Superlatives   ,,   like Bonus.

Compare :—

1. Clarus	Brevis	Prudens	Felix	Pulcher
2. Altus	Gravis	Potens	Ferox	Creber
3. Longus	Levis	Innocens	Velox	Aeger
4. Latus	Fortis	Recens	Ferax	Miser
5. Firmus	Fidelis	Patiens	Acer	Liber
6. Timidus	Crudelis	Ingens*	Celer	Asper

Decline the Comparatives and Superlatives of—
1. Clarus.   2. Brevis.   3. Prudens.
4. Felix.   5. Pulcher.   6. Miser.

---

* No Superlative.

17 (C). 1. Pulchrior soror brevius telum habet.
  2. Magister patientiorem puerum laudat.
  3. Aegri servi levissimum onus timent.
  4. Equitatus noster equos celerrimos habet.
  5. Brevissimi dies longiora itinera impediunt.
  6. Roma duces potentissimos habet.

  1. The longer arrows give more cruel wounds.
  2. The lords praise the more faithful slaves.
  3. A swifter chariot frightens the most timid soldiers.
  4. The army makes a longer march.
  5. The bravest men love peace.
  6. The most faithful slave kills the very fierce animal.

---

17 (D). 1. Milites muros urbium pulcherrimarum tenent.
  2. Faber telum puero fortiori dat.
  3. Liberi civium prudentiorum libros amant.
  4. Cives pontem navi celerrimā defendunt.
  5. Caesar rem duci prudentissimo credit.
  6. Equum vulnere graviore occidit.

  1. The brother praises the voice of the fairer sister.
  2. A stone wounds the head of the swiftest sailor.
  3. The lord gives a very fruitful field to the more faithful slave.
  4. The army of the bravest leader holds the mountain.
  5. The senate defends Rome with very high ramparts.
  6. The Gaul kills the lieutenant with a very hard blow.

Conjugation of Verbs.

18 (A). Verbs are **conjugated** by Voice, Mood, Tense, Number, and Person.

The **Voices** are **two,**—
  Active, as ămō, I love (*acting*)
  Passive, as ămŏr, I am loved (*acted upon*).

Verbs have **two Parts,**—Finite and Infinite.

The Verb **Finite** has **three Moods,**—
  The Indicative, which states a fact.
  The Conjunctive,   ,,   a possibility.
  The Imperative,   ,,   a command.

The Verb **Infinite** has the Infinitive Mood, with the Gerund, Supines, and Participles.

---

18 (B). The **Tenses** are **six,**—

  1. Present.   2. Future Simple.   3. Imperfect.
  4. Perfect.   5. Future Perfect.   6. Pluperfect.

The **Numbers** are **two,**—Singular and Plural.

Each Number has **three Persons,**—

SINGULAR.	PLURAL.
1st Person, **I** *	1st Person, **we**
2nd Person, **thou**	2nd Person, **ye** or **you**
3rd Person, **he, she, it**	3rd Person, **they**

Note.—The Present, Futures, and Perfect (with **have**) are called **Primary Tenses.**

The Imperfect, Pluperfect, and Perfect (without **have**) are called **Historic Tenses.**

---

* These Pronouns are implied in the Latin endings of **the** Tenses, the Latin Pronouns being used only when emphatic.

19 (A). Active Verbs are of **two kinds,—**
Transitive and **Intransitive.**

(1) Transitive, acting directly on an Object,—as

Subject.	Transitive Verb.	Object.
Magister	laudat	puerum
The master	*praises*	*the boy.*

(2) Intransitive (or Neuter), not acting directly on
an Object,—as

Subject.	Intransitive Verb.
Equus	currit
The horse	*runs.*

---

19 (B) **The Predicate.**

The Predicate **states** something about the Subject—
(1) what it is, (2) what it does, or (3) what is done
to it.

The Predicate is therefore commonly a Verb,—as

Subject.	Predicate.	Subject.	Predicate.
Magister	laudat.	Puer	laudatur.
The master	*praises.*	*The boy*	*is praised.*

But the Predicate may consist of a Noun or
Adjective, with the Verb Sum (*I am*),—as

Subject.	Predicate.	Subject.	Predicate.
Magister	est bonus.	Equus	est animal.
The master	*is good.*	*The horse*	*is an animal.*

The Verb **est** (*is*) is here called the **Copula** (or
Link), because it **links** the Subject to the Complement.

The Noun or Adjective is called the **Complement,**
because it **completes** the sense.

The Verb Sum (I am).

The Verb Sum is either Auxiliary or Copulative.

1. **Auxiliary,** when it **helps** to conjugate other Verbs.

2. **Copulative,** when it **links** the Subject to the
Complement.

20 (A). Principal Parts—Sum, essĕ, fŭī, fŭtūrŭs.

Indicative Mood.

Present Tense.

SINGULAR.	PLURAL.
sum, I am	sŭmŭs, we are
ĕs, thou art	estĭs, ye are
est, he is	sunt, they are

Future Simple Tense (*shall* or *will*).*

ĕr-ō, I shall be	ĕr-ĭmŭs, we shall be
ĕr-ĭs, thou wilt be	ĕr-ĭtĭs, ye will be
ĕr-ĭt, he will be	ĕr-unt, they will be

Imperfect Tense (*was*).

ĕr-am, I was	ĕr-āmŭs, we were
ĕr-ās, thou wast	ĕr-ātĭs, ye were
ĕr-ăt, he was	ĕr-ant, they were

---

20 (B).   Perfect Tense (*have*).

fŭ-ī, I have been†	fŭ-ĭmŭs, we have been
fŭ-istī, thou hast been	fŭ-istĭs, ye have been
fŭ-ĭt, he has been	fŭ-ērunt, or -ērĕ} they have been
† or, I was, thou wast, &c.	

Future Perfect Tense (*shall have*).

fŭ-ĕrō, I shall have ⎫	fŭ-ĕrimŭs, we shall have ⎫
fŭ-ĕris, thou wilt have ⎬ been	fŭ-ĕritĭs, ye will have ⎬ been
fŭ-ĕrĭt, he will have ⎭	fŭ-ĕrint, they will have ⎭

Pluperfect Tense (*had*).

fŭ-ĕram, I had been	fŭ-ĕrāmŭs, we had been
fŭ-ĕrās, thou hadst been	fŭ-ĕrātĭs, ye had been
fŭ-ĕrăt, he had been	fŭ-ĕrant, they had been

---

* The words *shall, was, have*, &c., are called the **Signs** of the Tenses. The Present has no Sign.

20 (C). *Rule* 4. The Complement agrees with the Subject,*—as

Subj.	Cop.	Comp.	Subj.	Cop.	Comp.
Urbs	est	magna	Equus	est	animal
The city	*is*	*great.*	*The horse*	*is*	*an animal.*

Say (or write) all the 3rd Persons (1) Singular, and (2) Plural, of the Indicative of Sum, with the English.

1. Frater est bonus.
2. Soror fuerat aegra.
3. Mare est altum.
4. Caesar dux clarus erat.
5. Magnae urbes pulchrae fuerunt.
6. Flumina magna erunt celeria.

1. The arrows were long.
2. The burden will be heavy.
3. The black horse was timid.
4. Timid animals are swift.
5. The sad slaves will have been innocent.
6. Galba has been a brave soldier.

---

20 (D). 1. Muri urbis altissimi sunt.
2. Casae militum fortes erant.
3. Soror Galbae felicissima erit.
4. Nomina ducum clariora fuerant.
5. Milites Galbae fideliores fuerint.
6. Naves hostium pulcherrimae fuerunt.

1. Galba was a friend of Caesar.
2. The fields of the Senones were fruitful.
3. The ramparts have been very strong.
4. The days will be very short.
5. Your sisters will have been very sick. [cruel.
6. The wounds of the short arrows had been more

---

* If the Complement is a Noun, in Case; if an Adjective, in Gender, Number, and Case.

21 (A).   Conjunctive Mood.

Present Tense (*may*).

SINGULAR.	PLURAL.
sim, I may be*	sīmŭs, we may be
sīs, thou mayst be	sītĭs, ye may be
sĭt, he may be	sint, they may be

Imperfect Tense (*might* or *would*).

ess-em,† I might be	ess-ēmŭs, we might be
ess-ēs, thou mightst be	ess-ētĭs, ye might be
ess-ĕt, he might be	ess-ent, they might be

† or, fŏrem, fŏrēs, fŏret, fŏrēmŭs, fŏrētĭs, fŏrent.

Perfect Tense (*may have*).

fŭ-ĕrim, I may		fŭ-ĕrimŭs, we may
fŭ-ĕris, thou mayst	have been	fŭ-ĕritĭs, ye may
tŭ-ĕrĭt, he may		fŭ-ĕrint, they may

(have been) (have been)

Pluperfect Tense (*should have* or *might have*).

fŭ-issem, I should		fŭ-issēmŭs, we should
fŭ-issēs, thou wouldst	have been	fŭ-issētĭs, ye would
fŭ-issĕt, he would		fŭ-issent, they would

(have been) (have been)

21 (B).   Imperative Mood.

Pres. ĕs, be thou		es-tĕ, be ye	
Fut. es-tŏ, thou must be		es-tōtĕ, ye must be	
es-tŏ, he must be		suntō, they must be	

VERB INFINITE.
Infinitive Mood.

Present and Imperfect, essĕ, to be.
Perfect and Pluperfect, fŭ-issĕ, to have been.
Future, fŭt-ūrŭs essĕ, or fŏrĕ, to be about to be.

Participle Future (like Bonus).

fŭtūr-ŭs, ă, um, about to be.

---

*Or, May I be, mayst thou be, &c., when used in a simple sentence.

21 (C). Say (or write) all the 3rd Persons (1) Singular, and (2) Plural, of the Conjunctive of Sum, with the English.

---

1. Frater sit prudens.
2. Oves essent timidae.
3. Moenia fuissent alta.
4. Puer bonus felix esto.
5. Mali cives miseri sunto.
6. Este patientes, amici.

1. May our life be long.
2. Your arrows may have been swift.
3. Great burdens would have been heavy.
4. The broad river might be deep.
5. O citizens, be ye free.
6. The slaves must be faithful.

---

21 (D). 1. Gladii hostium acerrimi fuissent.
2. Copiae Titi ingentes fuerint.
3. Victoria Caesaris clarior esset.
4. Portūs Gallorum meliores sint.
5. Galba, es prudentior.
6. Milites exercitūs vestri fortissimi sunto.

1. May the bodies of our soldiers be very strong.
2. The leaders of your army may have been prudent.
3. The friends of the innocent hostage would be sad.
4. Double lines-of-battle would have been stronger.
5. Our sailors must be brave.
6. O Caesar, Rome must be a free city.

22 (A). Repeat the rules for forming the Comparative and Superlative of Adjectives.

Decline together :—

1. Durior ictus.
2. Velocius telum.
3. Pulchrior dies.
4. Altissima turris.
5. Brevissimum iter.
6. Velocissimus currus.

22 (B). 1. Repeat the Verb Sum.

2. Explain the terms Predicate, Copula, and Complement.

---

22 (C). 1. Turres sunt altissimae.
2. Pernicies tristior fuisset.
3. Titus miles clarissimus erat.
4. Vulnera vestra asperrima fuerint.
5. Sagittae nostrae celeriores fuerunt.
6. Equus animal timidissimum est.

1. May our sailors be very brave.
2. Good boys will be happier.
3. Your cities might be fairer.
4. Our ships must be very swift.
5. O Galba, be thou a faithful friend.
6. Your towns had been stronger.

---

22 (D). 1. Legati amici ducis sint.
2. Portae arcis firmissimae sunto.
3. Onera servorum graviora fuerint.
4. Nomina virorum clarissima fuerant.
5. Impetus curruum crudelior erat.
6. Pericula belli ingentia essent.

1. Titus had been the lieutenant of Caesar.
2. The teeth of great animals are very hard.
3. The darts of the Gauls might be swifter.
4. The ramparts of your city must be strong.
5. O Titus, be thou a more prudent boy !
6. The sister of the soldier will be very sad.

23 (A).   The Four Conjugations.

There are **Four Conjugations** of Latin Verbs, known by the letter before -rĕ in the Infinitive.

The First Conjugation has ā (long) before rĕ,
         as ămā-rĕ, to love.

The Second Conjugation has ē (long) before rĕ,—
         as mŏnē-rĕ, to advise.

The Third Conjugation has ĕ (short)* before rĕ,–
         as rĕgĕ-rĕ, to rule.

The Fourth Conjugation has ī (long) before rĕ,—
         as audī-rĕ, to hear.

The letter before -rĕ (or -ĕrĕ)† in the Infinitive is called the **Character** of the Conjugation.

     I. A-verbs.   II. E-verbs.
     III. Consonant and U-verbs.   IV. I-verbs.

---

23 (B). The **Principal Parts** of a regular Verb are **four** :—

     1. Indicative Present.   2. Infinitive Present.
     3. Indicative Perfect.   4. Supine in -**um**.

as *Indic. Pres.*   ăm-ō,   I love.
    Infin. Pres.   ămā-rĕ,   to love.
    Indic. Perf.   ămāv-ī,   I have loved.
    Sup. in -um   ămāt-um,   to love.

By taking away the Endings -rĕ (or ĕrĕ),† -ī, -um, we get **three Stems**,—

     Present Stem.   *Perfect Stem.*   *Supine Stem.*
      ămā-   ămāv-   ămāt-

A **Clipt Stem** is a Stem without its Vowel Character, as *Present Stem*, ămā-, *Clipt Stem*, ăm-

These Stems are used to form the Tenses, &c., of the Verb.

---

* Preceded by a Consonant or U.   † In the Third Conjugation.

23 (C). Find the Stems of any Verbs in B 24—27.*

---

24 (B`   **First Conjugation** (like Amo).

	Ind. Pres.	Infin. Pres.	Ind. Perf.	Supine.
Usual form :	-ō,	-ārĕ,	-āvī,	-ātum.
1. Laud-ō,		-ārĕ,	-āvī,	-ātum, I praise
2. Port-ō,		-ārĕ,	-āvī,	-ātum, I carry.
3. Vast-ō,		-ārĕ,	-āvī,	-ātum, I lay waste.
4. Vulnĕr-ō,		-ārĕ,	-āvī,	-ātum, I wound.
5. Oppugn-ō,		-ārĕ,	-āvī,	-ātum, I attack, assault
6. Nuntĭ-ō,		-ārĕ,	-āvī,	-ātum, I announce.

---

25 (B).   **Second Conjugation** (like Moneo).

Usual form :	-ĕō,	-ērĕ,	-ŭī,	-ĭtum.
1. Hăb-ĕō,		-ērĕ,	-ŭī,	-ĭtum, I have.
2. Terr-ĕō,		-ērĕ,	-ŭī,	-ĭtum, I frighten.
3. Praeb-ĕō,		-ērĕ,	-ŭī,	-ĭtum, I afford, supply.
4. Dŏc-ĕō,		-ērĕ,	-ŭī,	-tum, I teach.
5. Tĕn-ĕō,		-ērĕ,	-ŭī,	-tum, I hold.
6. Tĭm-ĕō,		-ērĕ,	-ŭī,	—— I fear.

---

26 (B).   **Third Conjugation** (like Rego).

The Perfect and Supine are very irregular in formation.

1. Dūc-ō,	-ĕrĕ,	dux-ī,	duct-um, I lead, draw.
2. Cing-ō,	-ĕrĕ,	cinx-ī,	cinct-um, I surround.
3. Frang-ō,	-ĕrĕ,	frēg-ī,	fract-um, I break.
4. Vinc-ō,	-ĕrĕ,	vīc-ī,	vict-um, I conquer.
5. Mitt-ō,	-ĕrĕ,	mīs-ī,	miss-um, I send, throw.
6. Dēfend-ō,	-ĕrĕ,	dēfend-ī,	dēfens-um, I defend.

---

* It is not necessary to learn these Verbs until directions are given to do so in the following Exercises.

27-(B). Fourth Conjugation (like Audio).

Usual form : -ĭŏ, -īrĕ, -īvī (or -ĭī), -ītum.
1. Fīn-ĭŏ, -īrĕ, -īvī, -ītum, I finish, end.
2. Mūn-ĭŏ, -īrĕ, -īvī, -ītum, I fortify.
3. Pūn-ĭŏ, -īrĕ, -īvī, -ītum, I punish.
4. Custōd-ĭŏ, -īrĕ, -īvī, -ītum, I guard.
5. Impĕd-ĭŏ, -īrĕ, -īvī, -ītum, I hinder.
6. Apĕr-ĭŏ, -īrĕ, -ŭī, -tum, I open, disclose.

29 (B). All Conjugations.
1. Pugn-ŏ, -ārĕ, -āvī, -ātum, I fight.
2. Dŏ, dărĕ, dĕd-ī, dăt-um, I give.*
3. Instrŭ-ŏ, -ĕrĕ, -xī, -ctum, I draw up.
4. Vĭd-ĕŏ, -ērĕ, vĭd-ī, vīs-um, I see.
5. Claud-ŏ, -ĕrĕ, claus-ī, claus-um, I shut, close.
6. Vĕn-ĭŏ, -īrĕ, vēn-ī, vent-um, I come.

31 (B). 1. Păr-ŏ, -ārĕ, -āvī, -ātum, I prepare.
2. Jŭb-ĕŏ, -ērĕ, juss-ī, juss-um, I order, command.
3. Gĕr-ŏ, -ĕrĕ, gess-ī, gest-um, I carry on, wage.
4. Occīd-ŏ, -ĕrĕ, occīd-ī, occīs-um, I kill.
5. Pōn-ŏ, -ĕrĕ, pŏsŭ-ī, pŏsĭt-um, I place, pitch.
6. Constĭtŭ-ŏ, -ĕrĕ, -ī, constĭtūt-um, I determine,
appoint.

41 (B). Third Conjugation, in -io.
1. Jăc-ĭŏ, -ĕrĕ, jēc-ī, jact-um, I throw, cast.
2. Făc-ĭŏ, -ĕrĕ, fēc-ī, fact-um, I make, do.
3. Confĭc-ĭŏ, -ĕrĕ, confēc-ī, confect-um, I finish.
4. Interfĭc-ĭŏ, -ĕrĕ, interfēc-ī, interfect-um, I kill.
5. Accĭp-ĭŏ, -ĕrĕ, accēp-ī, accept-um, I receive.
6. Fŭg-ĭŏ, -ĕrĕ, fŭg-ī, fŭgĭt-um, I flee, fly.

---

* **Do** belongs to the First Conjugation, but has ă (short) before **re**.

24 (A).   ACTIVE VOICE.

ăm-ō, ămā-rĕ, ămāv-ī, ămāt-um, *I love.*

Pres. Stem., ămā-, *Perf. Stem.,* ămāv-, *Sup. Stem.,* **ămāt-.**

Indicative Mood.*

Present Tense (*Clipt Stem*).

SINGULAR.	PLURAL.
ăm-ō, I love	ăm-āmŭs, we love
ăm-ās, thou lovest	ăm-ātĭs, ye love
ăm-ăt, he loves	ăm-ant, they love

Future Simple Tense (*Pres. Stem*).

ămā-bō, I shall	} love	ămā-bĭmŭs, we shall	} love
ămā-bĭs, thou wilt		ămā-bĭtĭs, ye will	
ămā-bĭt, he will		ămā-bunt, they will	

Imperfect Tense (*Pres. Stem*).

ămā-bam, I was	} loving	ămā-bāmŭs, we were	} loving
ămā-bās, thou wast		ămā-bātĭs, ye were	
ămā-băt, he was		ămā-bant, they were	

Perfect Tense (*Perfect Stem*).

ămāv-ī, I have†	} loved	ămāv-ĭmŭs, we have	} loved
ămāv-istī, thou hast		ămāv-istĭs, ye have	
ămāv-ĭt, he has		ămāv-ērunt or -ērĕ } they have	

† or, I loved, thou lovedst, &c.

Future Perfect Tense (*Perf. Stem*).

ămāv-ĕrō, I shall	} have loved	ămāv-ĕrimŭs, we shall	} have loved
ămāv-ĕris, thou wilt		ămāv-ĕritĭs, ye will	
ămāv-ĕrĭt, he will		ămāv-ĕrint, they will	

Pluperfect Tense (*Perf. Stem*).

ămāv-ĕram, I had	} loved	ămāv ĕrāmŭs, we had	} loved
ămāv-ĕrās, thou hadst		ămāv-ĕrātĭs, ye had	
ămāv-ĕrăt, he had		ămāv-ĕrant, they had	

* *Note.*—The Endings of the Future Simple and Imperfect are the same as in Sum, with **b** prefixed. The Endings of the Perfect-stem Tenses are the same as in Sum. The Signs are the same as in Sum.

24 (B). 1. Learn the Principal Parts (p. 44) of :—

 1. **Laudo.** 2. **Porto.** 3. **Vasto.**
 4. **Vulnero.** 5. **Oppugno.** 6. **Nuntio.**

 2. Find their Stems, and conjugate them like Amo

 3. Give all the 3rd Persons—(1) Singular. and (2) Plural, with the English.

---

24 (C). 1. Magister pueros laudat.
 2. Servi onera portabant.
 3. Galli agros vastabunt.
 4. Caesar oppidum oppugnavit.
 5. Legati rem nuntiaverant.
 6. Hostes civem vulneraverint.

 1. The senate was praising the army.
 2. The standard-bearer will announce the danger.
 3. The enemy had attacked the city.
 4. The Cimbri will have laid-waste the fields.
 5. The horse carries a burden.
 6. An arrow wounded the standard-bearer.

---

24 (D). 1. Viri omnes impetum equitatūs laudabant.
 2. Dux Gallorum muros nostros oppugnat.
 3. Nautae timidi longa retia portaverant.
 4. Ictus hostium milites nostros vulnerabunt.
 5. Galba rem civibus miseris nuntiavit.
 6. Hostes urbem igne vastant.

 1. Immense forces of the enemy assaulted the town.
 2. The soldiers of Titus were carrying small shields.
 3. The garrison had wounded our soldiers with stones.
 4. The lieutenant announces to Caesar the approach of the Gauls.
 5. The lords will have praised the faith of the slaves.
 6. The cavalry had laid waste the plain with cruel war.

25 (A).   ACTIVE VOICE.

mŏn-ĕō, mŏnē-rĕ, mŏnŭ-ī, mŏnĭt-um, I advise.

Pres. Stem, mŏnē-; *Perf. Stem,* mŏnŭ-; *Sup. Stem,* mŏnĭt-.

Indicative Mood.*

Present Tense (*Clipt Stem*).

SINGULAR.	PLURAL.
mŏn-ĕō, I advise	mŏn-ēmŭs, we advise
mŏn-ēs, thou advisest	mŏn-ētĭs, ye advise
mŏn-ĕt, he advises	mŏn-ent, they advise

Future Simple Tense (*Pres. Stem*).

mŏnē-bō, I shall	} advise	mŏnē-bĭmŭs, we shall	} advise
mŏnē-bĭs, thou wilt		mŏnē-bĭtĭs, ye will	
mŏnē-bĭt, he will		mŏnē-bunt, they will	

Imperfect Tense (*Pres. Stem*).

mŏnē-bam, I was	} advising	mŏnē-bāmŭs, we were	} advising
mŏnē-bās, thou wast		mŏnē-bātĭs, ye were	
mŏnē-băt, he was		mŏnē-bant, they were	

Perfect Tense (*Perf. Stem*).

mŏnŭ-ī, I have†	} advised	mŏnŭ-ĭmŭs, we have	} advised
mŏnŭ-istī, thou hast		mŏnŭ-istĭs, ye have	
mŏnŭ-ĭt, he has		mŏnŭ-ērunt } they have or -ērĕ	

† or, I advised, thou advisedst, &c.

Future Perfect Tense (*Perf. Stem*).

mŏnŭ-ĕrō, I shall	} have advised	mŏnŭ-ĕrimŭs, we shall	} have advised
mŏnŭ-ĕris, thou wilt		mŏnŭ-ĕritĭs, ye will	
mŏnŭ-ĕrĭt, he will		mŏnŭ-ĕrint, they will	

Pluperfect Tense (*Perf. Stem*).

mŏnŭ-ĕram, I had	} advised	mŏnŭ-ĕrāmŭs, we had	} advised
mŏnŭ-ĕrās, thou hadst		mŏnŭ-ĕrātĭs, ye had	
mŏnŭ-ĕrăt, he had		mŏnŭ-ĕrant, they had	

* *Note.*—The Endings are the same as in Amo, except in the Present.

25 (B). 1. Learn the Principal Parts (p. 44) of
    1. **Habeo.**   2. **Terreo.**   3. **Praebeo.**
    4. **Doceo.**   5. **Teneo.**   6. **Timeo.**

  2. Find their Stems, and conjugate them like Moneo.

  3. Give all the 3rd Persons—(1) Singular, and (2) Plural, with the English.

---

25 (C). 1. Miles gladium habet.
  2. Servi dominos timebant.
  3. Galli Romam tenebunt.
  4. Sagittae hostes terruerant.
  5. Victoria spem praebuit.
  6. Magistri pueros docuerint.

  1. The hostages will fear Caesar.
  2. The boy was holding the book.
  3. The fields supply sheep.
  4. Nets will have frightened the horses.
  5. The animals had wounds.
  6. The father-in-law has taught the son-in-law.

---

25 (D). 1. Timidi cives pericula belli timuerint.
  2. Caesar Gallos feroces specie pugnae terruerat.
  3. Nautae navem longo fune tenebant.
  4. Urbs duci claro milites praebebit.
  5. Pulchra soror amicum Galbae docet.
  6. Corpora animalium vulnera gravia habuerunt.

  1. High mountains will frighten the leader of the Cimbri.
  2. The approach of the cavalry supplies hope to the wretched Senones.
  3. All the men feared the teeth of the fierce animals.
  4. The voice of the friend will teach the children.
  5. The towns of Kent had had brave citizens.
  6. The Cimbri will have held the plain with a great army.

E

26 (A).   ACTIVE VOICE.

rĕg-ō, rĕg-ĕrĕ, rēx-ī, rect-um, I rule.

Pres. Stem, rĕg-, *Perf. Stem,* rēx-, *Sup. Stem,* rect-.

Indicative Mood.*

Present Tense (*Pres. Stem*).

SINGULAR.	PLURAL.
rĕg-ō, I rule	rĕg-ĭmŭs, we rule
rĕg-ĭs, thou rulest.	rĕg-ĭtĭs, ye rule
rĕg-ĭt, he rules	rĕg-unt, they rule

Future Simple Tense (*Pres. Stem*).

rĕg-am, I shall	rĕg-ēmŭs, we shall	
rĕg-ēs, thou wilt } rule	rĕg-ētĭs, ye will	} rule
rĕg-ĕt, he will	rĕg-ent, they will	

Imperfect Tense (*Pres. Stem* with ē).

rĕg-ē-bam, I was	rĕg-ē-bāmŭs, we were	
rĕg-ē-bās, thou wast } ruling	rĕg-ē-bātĭs, ye were	} ruling
rĕg-ē-băt, he was	rĕg-ē-bant, they were	

Perfect Tense (*Perf. Stem*).

rēx-ī, I have †	rēx-ĭmŭs, we have	
rēx-istī, thou hast } ruled	rēx-istĭs, ye have	} ruled
rēx-ĭt, he has	rēx-ērunt } they have or -ērĕ }	

† or, I ruled, thou ruledst, &c.

Future Perfect Tense (*Perf. Stem*).

rēx-ĕrŏ, I shall	rēx-ĕrimŭs, we shall	
rēx-ĕris, thou wilt } have ruled	rēx-ĕritĭs, ye will	} have ruled
rēx-ĕrĭt, he will	rēx-ĕrint, they will	

Pluperfect Tense (*Perf. Stem*).

rēx-ĕram, I had	rēx-ĕrāmŭs, we had	
rēx-ĕrās, thou hadst } ruled	rēx-ĕrātĭs, ye had	} ruled
rēx-ĕrăt, he had	rēx-ĕrant, they had	

---

* *Note.*—The Tense-endings are the same as in Moneo, except in the Present and Future Simple.

26 (B). Learn the Principal Parts (p. 44) of
    1. **Duco.**   2. **Cingo.**   3. **Frango.**
    4. **Vinco.**   5. **Mitto.**   6. **Defendo**
  2. Find their Stems, and conjugate them like Rego.
  3. Give all the 3rd Persons—(1) Singular, and
(2) Plural, with the English.

---

26 (C). 1. Titus omnem equitatum mittit.
  2. Hostes montem cinxerunt.
  3. Praesidium castra defendebat.
  4. Consules Gallos vicerint.
  5. Servus sagittam franget.
  6. Caesar ingentes copias duxerat.

  1. A broad river surrounds the town.
  2. Our cavalry will defend the gates.
  3. Your armies were conquering the Cimbri.
  4. The sea had broken the ships.
  5. Swift horses will have drawn the chariots.
  6. The senate has sent a lieutenant.

---

26 (D). 1. Cives urbem moenibus altis cinxerant.
  2. Titus spes Gallorum crebris bellis fregit.
  3. Frater sororem teneram gladio defendet.
  4. Caesar Senones acri pugna vicit.
  5. Amicus innocentis pueri equum ducebat.
  6. Oppida Cantii naves celerrimas miserint.

  1. The Gauls were surrounding the camp of Caesar.
  2. All the sailors had defended the harbour with swift ships.
  3. Our soldiers will have conquered the armies of the enemy (*pl.*)
  4. They have broken the gates of the high city with heavy blows.
  5. The consul leads the army of faithful citizens.
  6. The leader of the Senones will send hostages.

27 (A).   ACTIVE VOICE.

aud-ĭŏ, audī-rĕ, audīv-ī, audīt-um, I hear.

Pres. Stem, audi-; *Perf. Stem,* audīv-; *Sup. Stem,* audīt-

Indicative Mood.*

Present Tense (*Clipt Stem*).

SINGULAR.	PLURAL.
aud-ĭŏ, I hear	aud-ĭmŭs, we hear
aud-īs, thou hearest	aud-ītĭs, ye hear
aud-ĭt, he hears	aud-ĭunt, they hear

Future Simple Tense (*Pres. Stem*).

audĭ-am, I shall ⎫	audĭ-ēmŭs, we shall ⎫
audĭ-ēs, thou wilt ⎬ hear	audĭ-ētĭs, ye will ⎬ hear
audĭ-ĕt, he will ⎭	audĭ-ent, they will ⎭

Imperfect Tense (*Pres. Stem,* with ē).

audĭ-ē-bam, I was ⎫	audĭ-ē-bāmŭs, we were ⎫
audĭ-ē-bās, thou wast ⎬ hearing	audĭ-ē-bātĭs, ye were ⎬ hearing
audĭ-ē-băt, he was ⎭	audĭ-ē-bant, they were ⎭

Perfect Tense (*Perf. Stem*).

audīv-ī, I have† ⎫	audīv-ĭmŭs, we have ⎫
audīv-istī, thou hast ⎬ heard	audīv-istĭs, ye have ⎬ heard
audīv-ĭt, he has ⎭	audīv-ērunt ⎱ they have ⎭
	or -ērĕ ⎰

† or, I heard, thou heardest, &c.

Future Perfect Tense (*Perf. Stem*).

audīv-ĕrŏ, I shall ⎫	audīv-ĕrimŭs, we shall ⎫
audīv-ĕris, thou wilt ⎬ have heard	audīv-ĕritĭs, ye will ⎬ have heard
audīv-ĕrĭt, he will ⎭	audīv-ĕrint, they will ⎭

Pluperfect Tense (*Perf. Stem*).

audīv-ĕram, I had ⎫	audīv-ĕrāmŭs, we had ⎫
audīv-ĕrās, thou hadst ⎬ heard	audīv-ĕrātĭs, ye had ⎬ heard
audīv-ĕrăt, he had ⎭	audīv-ĕrant, they had ⎭

* *Note.*—The Endings are the same as in Rego, except in the Present.
Rego and Audio add -e to the Present Stem in the Imperfect.

27 (B). 1. Learn the Principal Parts (p. 45) of
   1. Finio.   2. Munio.   3. Punio.
   4. Custodio.   5. Impedio.   6. Aperio.
  2. Find their Stems, and conjugate them like Audio.
  3. Give all the 3rd Persons—(1) Singular, and (2) Plural, with the English.

27 (C). 1. Magister malos pueros puniet.
  2. Milites fortes moenia custodiunt.
  3. Caesar castra muniverat.
  4. Onera magna servos impediebant.
  5. Pax bellum finiverit.
  6. Cives boni arbitros audiunt.

  1. The Cimbri were fortifying the towns.
  2. Our cavalry has hindered the enemy.
  3. Titus finished the fierce battle.
  4. A lieutenant had punished the timid soldier.
  5. The patient boys will open the book.
  6. The prudent leaders will have guarded the hostages.

27 (D). 1. Parvus puer oves domini custodiverat.
  2. Boni cives urbem moenibus altis muniverint.
  3. Consul liberos civium innocentium puniebat.
  4. Niger servus portas urbis Gallis aperuit.
  5. Maria adventum hostium nostrorum impediunt.
  6. Puer nomina virorum clarissimorum audiet.

  1. Caesar fortifies the citadel with high towers.
  2. The brave sailors will guard the bridge with ships.
  3. The friend of the cruel lord punished the sick slave.
  4. The Gauls had hindered the army of Caesar with frequent stones.   [Titus.
  5. The Cimbri will open the gates of the town to
  6. The sister of the sailor was finishing the long net.

28 (A.)   **Indicative Mood.**

Pres. Stem.		Present Tense.					
1. Am-	ō	ās	ăt	āmŭs	ātĭs	ant	1. I love, &c.
2. Mŏn-	ĕō	ēs	ĕt	ēmŭs	ētĭs	ent	2. I advise,&c.
3. Rĕg-	ō	ĭs	ĭt	ĭmŭs	ĭtĭs	unt	3. I rule, &c.
4. Aud-	ĭō	īs	ĭt	īmŭs	ītĭs	ĭunt	4. I hear, &c.

Pres. Stem.		Future Simple Tense.			
1. Amā-	bō bĭs	3. Rĕg-	am, I shall ēs, thou wilt	1. love
2. Mŏnē-	bĭt bĭmŭs bĭtĭs bunt	4. Audĭ-	ĕt, he will ēmŭs, we shall ētĭs, ye will ent, they will	2. advise 3. rule 4. hear

Pres. Stem.	Imperfect Tense.	
1. Amā-	bam, I was bās, thou wast	1. loving
2. Mŏnē-	băt, he was	2. advising
3. Rĕg-ē-	bāmŭs, we were bātĭs, ye were	3. ruling
4. Audĭ-ē-	bant, they were	4. hearing

Perf. Stem.	Perf.	Fut. Perf.	Pluperf.	
1. Amāv-	ī istī	ĕrō ĕris	ĕram ĕrās	1. loved
2. Mŏnŭ-	ĭt	ĕrĭt	ĕrăt	2. advised
3. Rex-	ĭmŭs istĭs	ĕrimŭs ĕritĭs	ĕrāmŭs ĕrātĭs	3. ruled
4. Audīv-	ērunt or ērĕ	ĕrint	ĕrant	4. heard

(Perf. col: I have, &c.) (Fut. Perf. col: I shall have, &c.) (Pluperf. col: I had, &c.)

28 (B). Repeat the Principal Parts, and conjugate the Indicative Mood of any Verbs in B (24—27).

---

28 (C). 1. Bonus frater sororem parvam docuit.
2. Currus celerrimi equos fortiores habebant.
3. Domini potentissimi servos miserrimos puniverint.
4. Hostes vestri latos agros vastaverant.
5. Feroces Cimbri exercitum magnum ducent.
6. Magistri patientes puerum felicissimum laudabunt.

1. The patient slaves will carry the heaviest burdens.
2. The strong man will break a harder dart.
3. Prudent men have sent more beautiful books.
4. Fierce Gauls had attacked the firmest citadels.
5. The swiftest ships surrounded the great harbour.
6. Peace will have ended the sad war.

---

28 (D). 1. Consules urbem moenibus altis muniebant.
2. Galba rem civibus miserrimis nuntiat.
3. Dux fortis milites timidos voce magna terruerat.
4. Fabri dentes animalium ferocium timebunt.
5. Velocius telum caput Galbae vulneravit.
6. Nautae naves funibus longissimis tenuerint.

1. Swifter rivers will hinder the march of the Cimbri.
2. The sad citizens had opened the gates of the city.
3. The garrison will have defended the town with stones.
4. Our soldiers have conquered the armies of the enemy.
5. A small victory affords great hope to the leader
6. Good leaders will guard the gates of the city.

29 (A). **Conjunctive Mood.***

Clipt Stem.	Pres. Stem.	Present Tense (*may*).	
1. Am-em	2. Mŏnĕ-	am, I may†	1. love
Am-ēs		ās, thou mayst	
Am-ĕt	3. Rĕg-	ăt, he may	2. advise
Am-ēmŭs		āmus, we may	
Am-ĕtĭs	4. Audĭ-	ătĭs, ye may	3. rule
Am-ĕnt		ant, they may	4. hear

† or, May I, mayst thou, &c.

Pres. Stem.	Imperfect Tense (*might* or *should*).	
1. Amā-	rem, I might	1. love
	rēs, thou mightst	
2. Mŏnē-	rĕt, he might	2. advise
3. Rĕg-ĕ-	rēmŭs, we might	3. rule
	rētĭs, ye might	
4. Audĭ-	rent, they might	4. hear

Perf. Stem.	Perfect Tense (*may have*).	
1. Amāv-	ĕrim, I may have	1. loved
	ĕris, thou mayst have	
2. Mŏnŭ-	ĕrĭt, he may have	2. advised
3. Rēx-	ĕrĭmŭs, we may have	3. ruled
	ĕritĭs, ye may have	
4. Audĭv-	ĕrint, they may have	4. heard

Perf. Stem.	Pluperfect Tense (*should* or *might have*).	
1. Amāv-	issem, I should have	1. loved
	issés, thou wouldst have	
2. Mŏnŭ-	issĕt, he would have	2. advised
3. Rēx-	issēmŭs, we should have	3. ruled
	issētĭs, ye would have	
4. Audĭv-	issent, they would have	4. heard

* Called Subjunctive when subjoined to another Verb.

29 (B). 1. Learn the Principal Parts (p. 45) of

1. Pugno.	2. Do.	3. Instruo.
4. Video.	5. Claudo.	6. Venio.

2. Say to which Conjugation each belongs, and give the Stems.

3. Give all the 3rd Persons (1) Singular, and (2) Plural, of the Indicative and Conjunctive, with the English.

---

29 (C). *Rule* 5. The Conjunctions **ŭt,** *that,* **nē,** *lest,* take the Subjunctive.

1. Puer venit, ut videat.
2. Hostes pugnabunt, ut vincant.
3. Cives timebant, ne pugnarent.
4. Aciem instruit, ut pugnet.
5. Magister pueros malos punivisset.
6. Mare naves magnas freç erit.

1. We will come, that we may hear.
2. They were fighting, that they might conquer.
3. He had come. that he might see.
4. We feared, lest ye might come.
5. Chariots would have surrounded the city.
6. The arrows may have frightened the enemy.

---

29 (D). Dux milites laudat, ut vincat.
2. Caesar equitatum misit, ut agros nostros vastet.
3. Galli agmina ducebant, ut Romam cingerent.
4. Cives portas clauserunt, ne hostes urbem oppug-narent.
5. Titus praesidium misisset, ut castra defen-deret.
3. Copias magnas instruxerant, ne hostes venirent.

1. The lieutenant was coming, that he might announce the victory.
2. The Cimbri fear, lest Caesar may attack the
villages.
3. The Gauls came, that they might see the city.
4. Ships will come, that they may guard the bridge.
5. They would have fought, that they might conquer.
6. The Senones have given hostages, lest Titus
may lay-waste the fields.

30 (A). Imperative Mood (*Clipt Stem*).

	PRESENT TENSE.	FUTURE TENSE.	
S. 2.	Am-ā, love **thou**	Am-ātō, thou must	
3.		ātō, he must	
P. 2.	ātĕ, love **ye**	ātōtĕ, ye must	love.
3.		antō, they must	
S. 2.	Mŏn-ē, advise **thou**	Mŏn-ētō, thou must	
3.		ētō, he must	
P. 2.	ētĕ, advise **ye**	ētōtĕ, ye must	advise.
3.		entō, they must	
S. 2.	Rĕg-ĕ, rule **thou**	Rĕg-ĭtō, thou must	
3.		ĭtō, he must	
P. 2.	ĭtĕ, rule **ye**	ĭtōtĕ, ye must	rule.
3.		untō, they must	
S. 2.	Aud-ī, hear **thou**	Aud-ītō, thou must	
3.		ītō, he must	
P. 2.	ītĕ, hear **ye**	ītōtĕ, ye must	hear.
3.		ĭuntō, they must	

Note.—Duco, dico, and facio, drop ĕ in the Imperative Present
2nd Pers. Sing., and make duc, dic, and fac.

30 (B). Say the Imperative Mood of any of the Verbs
in B (24—29).

---

30 (C). 1. Pueri, amate fratres vestros.
2. Magister puerum moneto.
3. Urbem vestram munitote, cives.
4. Hostes bellum finiunto.
5. Castra defendite, milites.
6. Aciem duplicem instruunto.

1. Hear ye, O slaves.
2. Soldiers, break ye your darts.
3. The master must teach the boys.
4. Come thou, O Titus.
5. Announce ye the thing to your leader.
6. They must guard the sacred citadel.

---

30 (D). 1. Venite, ut pugnam videatis.
2. Portas clauditote, ne Galli oppidum vastent.
3. Duplicem aciem instrue, ut urbem defendas.
4. Servum moneto, ut portas claudat.
5. Portum tenete, ne mare naves frangat.
6. Cives pugnanto, ut Gallos vincant.

1. Fight thou, that thou mayst conquer.
2. Ye must fortify the town, lest Caesar may come.
3. Send ye Galba, that he may hold the mountain.
4. Masters must punish bad boys.
5. Thou must praise the soldier, that he may fight.
6. They must come that they may hear.

31 (A).   **VERB INFINITE.**
                 Infinitive Mood.

Pres. Stem. Pres. & Imperf.		*Perf. Stem.*	Perf. & Pluperf.
1. Amā- 2. Mŏnē- 3. Rĕg-ĕ- 4. Audī-	rĕ, to — 1. love 2. advise 3. rule 4. hear	1. Amāv- 2. Mŏnŭ- 3. Rēx- 4. Audīv-	issĕ, to have — 1. loved 2. advised 3. ruled 4. heard

Sup. Stem.	Future.	
1. Amāt- 2. Mŏnĭt- 3. Rect- 4. Audīt-	-ūrŭs essĕ, to be about to	1. love 2. advise 3. rule 4. hear

Gerund (like Bellum).

1. Am-and- 2. Mŏn-end- 3. Rĕg-end- 4. Aud-ĭend-	um, — ī, of ŏ, to ō, by	1. loving 2. advising 3. ruling 4. hearing

Sup. Stem. Supine in -um.		*Sup. Stem.*	Supine in -u.
1. Amāt- 2. Mŏnĭt- 3. Rect- 4. Audīt-	um, to — 1. love 2. advise 3. rule 4. hear	1. Amāt- 2. Mŏnĭt- 3. Rect- 4. Audīt-	ū, to be — 1. loved 2. advised 3. ruled 4. heard

Participles.

Present (like Ingens).   *Sup. Stem.*   Future (like Bonus).

1. Am-ans, lov-ing 2. Mŏn-ens, advis-ing 3. Rĕg-ens, rul-ing 4. Aud-ĭens, hear-ing	1. Amāt- 2. Mŏnĭt- 3. Rect- 4. Audīt-	ūrŭs, about to — 1. love 2. advise 3. rule 4 hear

31 (B). 1. Learn the Principal Parts (p. 45) of

    1. Paro.   2. Jubeo.   3. Pono.

    4. Gero.   5. Occīdo.   6. Constituo.

    2. Give all the 3rd Persons (1) Singular, and (2) Plural.

    3. Repeat the Verb Infinite of any Verbs in B (24—31).

---

31 (C). *Rule* 6. The Infinitive carries on the construction of a Verb or Adjective.

    1. Consul castra ponere parat.

    2. Caesar aciem instruere parabat.

    3. Dominus servum portas aperire jusserat.

    4. Duces bellum gerere constituerunt.

    5. Consules aciem cingere montem jubent.

    6. Cimbri pugnare timuerant.

    1. The master orders the boy to come.

    2. The slave was fearing to carry the burden.

    3. Our leader ordered the soldier to kill the hostage.

    4. The enemy (*pl.*) prepared to assault the village.

    5. Galba determined to lay waste the plain.

    6. The senate had determined to wage war.

---

31 (D). 1. Praesidium portas castrorum custodire paraverat.

    2. Concilium urbem moenibus defendere constituit.

    3. Dux legatum victoriam civibus nuntiare jubebit.

    4. Caesar Gallos gladiis occidere paravit.

    5. Consul urbem muro altissimo cingere constituet.

    6. Galli obsides Caesari dare timent.

    1. The lord ordered the slaves to draw the waggon.

    2. The citizens determine to fortify the town with towers

3. The forces of the Cimbri will prepare to pitch the camp.
4. The Gauls had prepared to break the gates of the city.
5. The Senones were preparing to give hostages to Caesar.
6. Titus determined to lay waste the fields with fire.

Questions on the Active Voice.

32 (A). 1. How many Conjugations are there, and how are they distinguished? Give examples.
2. Name the Principal Parts of a Verb Active. Give examples.
3. How many Stems have Verbs, and how may they be found?
4. Which Tenses are formed with the Present (or Clipt) Stem, and which with the Perfect Stem?
5. Give the Signs of the Tenses in the Indicative and Conjunctive Mood.
6. What is the difference between a Transitive and an Intransitive (or Neuter) Verb? Give examples.
7. Repeat the whole of the Active Voice of the Four Conjugations.

---

32 (B). 1. Give the 3rd Persons (1) Singular, and (2) Plural of the Indicative and Conjunctive of **any** Verbs in B (24—31).
2. Say the Imperative and Infinitive Moods of
  1. **Nuntio.** 2. **Habeo.** 3. **Cingo.** 4. **Punio.**
  5. **Do.**   6. **Video.** 7. **Duco.** 8. **Venio.**
3. What Mood do **ut**, *that*, and **ne**, *lest*, govern?
4. Give the rule for the use of the Infinitive.

82 (C). 1. Magister prudens malos pueros puniet.
2. Galli pugnaverunt, ut Caesarem vincerent.
3. Bellum parate, ut pacem habeatis.
4. Hostes tela mittere paraverant, ut ducem nostrum vulnerarent.　　·
5. Galba milites castra ponere jussit.
6. Praesidium venisset, ut oppidum custodiret.

1. The boys will come, that they may see the battle.
2. The lord will have praised the faithful slaves.
3. The sailors were fearing, lest the sea might break the small ship.
4. An immense army had held the broad plain.
5. Caesar determined to finish the long war.
6. O master, come, that thou mayst teach the boy.

---

82 (D). 1. Titus castra praesidio defendere constituit.
2. Caesar copias ducebat, ut urbes pulcherrimas Gallorum vastaret.　　　　　　[venirent.
3 Senatus portas castrorum clausit, ne hostes
4. Dux legatum mittet, ut rem Caesari nuntiet.
5. Plebes urbem moenibus munire paraverat.
6. Cives, urbem vestram muro cingitote, ne hostes oppugnent.

1. Caesar will wage war, that he may frighten the Cimbri.
2. The Senones would have given hostages to Titus.
3. The Gaul had feared, lest Caesar might kill the leader with a sword.　　·
4. The enemy (*pl.*) were drawing up an immense army (in line), that they might hinder the approach of Titus.
5. O slave, come thou, that thou mayst carry the heavy burden.
6. The consul will fear to open the gates of the citadel

33 (A).   PASSIVE VOICE.

Indic. Pres.   Infin. Pres.   Partic. Perf.

Principal Parts, ăm-ŏr, ămā-rī, ămāt-ŭs, **I am loved.**

Indicative Mood.

Present Tense (*Clipt Stem*).

SINGULAR.	PLURAL.
ăm-ŏr, I am loved	ăm-āmŭr, we are loved
ăm-arĭs,* thou art loved	ăm-āmĭnī, ye are loved
ăm-ātŭr, he is loved	ăm-antŭr, they are loved

Future Simple Tense (*Pres. Stem*).

ămā-bŏr, I shall be	⎱ loved	ămā-bĭmŭr, we shall be ⎱ loved
ămā-bĕrĭs,* thou wilt be		ămā-bĭmĭnī, ye will be
ămā-bĭtŭr, he will be		ămā-buntŭr, they will be

Imperfect Tense (*Pres. Stem*).

ămā-băr, I was	⎱ being loved	ămā-bāmŭr, we were ⎱ being loved
ămā-bārĭs,* thou wast		ămā-bāmĭnī, ye were
ămā-bātŭr, he was		ămā-bantŭr, they were

Perfect Tense (*Supine Stem*).

ămāt-ŭs‡ sum, I was†	⎱ loved	ămāt-ī sŭmŭs, we were ⎱ loved
ămāt-ŭs ĕs, thou wast		ămāt-ī estĭs, ye were
ămāt-ŭs ĕst, he was		ămāt-ī sunt, they were

† or, I have been, thou hast been, &c.

Future Perfect Tense (*Sup. Stem*).

ămāt-ŭs ĕrō, I shall	⎱ have been loved	ămāt-ī ĕrĭmŭs, we shall ⎱ have been loved
ămāt-ŭs ĕrĭs, thou wilt		ămāt-ī ĕrĭtĭs, ye will
ămāt-ŭs ĕrĭt, he will		ămāt-ī ĕrunt, they will

Pluperfect Tense (*Sup. Stem*).

ămāt-ŭs ĕram, I had	⎱ been loved	ămāt-ī ĕrāmŭs, we had ⎱ been loved
ămāt-ŭs ĕrās, thou hadst		ămāt-ī ĕrātĭs, ye had
ămāt-ŭs ĕrăt, he had		ămāt-ī ĕrant, they had

* -ĭs, or -ĕ. ‡ Amatus is declined like **Bonus, and agrees with its** Nominative in Gender, Number, and Case.

33 (B). 1. Conjugate like Amor the Passive of :—
   1. **Laudo.**   2. **Porto.**   3. **Vasto.**
   4. **Vulnero.**   5. **Oppugno.**   6. **Nuntio.**
   2. Give all the 3rd Persons—(1) Singular, and (2) Plural, with the English.

---

33 (C) *Rule* 7.—The Ablative of the Agent, By whom?
   requires the Preposition **a** or **ab*** (by) before it.
1. Bonus puer laudatur.
2. Agri feraces vastabantur.
3. Magnum onus portabitur.
4. Res nuntiatae erant.
5. Oppida magna a Tito oppugnata sunt.
6. Cives timidi ab hostibus vulnerati erunt.

1. Caesar will be praised.
2. The danger was being announced.
3. The fair city had been assaulted.
4. Our fields will have been laid-waste.
5. A very heavy burden is carried by the horse.
6. Your friend has been wounded by the Gauls.

---

33 (D). 1. Impetus curruum a Caesare laudabatur.
2. Moenia vestra ab exercitu Senonum oppugnantur.
3. Longa retia a servis portata erant.
4. Milites nostri ictibus hostium vulnerati sunt.
5. Pernicies aciei civibus miseris nuntiata erit.
6. Urbs pulcherrima igne vastabitur.

1. The camp of the Cimbri will have been assaulted by Galba.
2. Small shields were carried by the soldiers of Titus.
3. The approach of the Gauls is announced to Caesar.
4. Faithful slaves have been praised by the lords.
5. The sick hostage had been wounded by the garrison.
6. The great plain will be laid-waste by the cavalry.

* **a** is generally used before a Consonant and **ab** before a Vowel, or h.

F

34 (A).   PASSIVE VOICE.

mŏn-ĕŏr, mŏnē-rī, mŏnĭt-ŭs, I am advised.

Indicative Mood.‡

Present Tense (*Clipt Stem*).

SINGULAR.	PLURAL.
mŏn-ĕŏr, I am advised	mŏn-ēmŭr, we are advised
mŏn-ērĭs,* thou art advised	mŏn-ēmĭnī, ye are advised
mŏn-ētŭr, he is advised	mŏn-entŭr, they are advised

Future Simple Tense (*Pres. Stem*).

mŏnē-bŏr, I shall be	mŏnē-bĭmŭr, we shall be	
mŏnē-bĕrĭs,*thou wilt be } advised	mŏnē-bĭmĭnī, ye will be } advised
mŏnē-bĭtŭr, he will be	mŏnē-buntŭr, they will be

Imperfect Tense (*Pres. Stem*).

mŏnē-băr, I was	mŏnē-bāmŭr, we were	
mŏnē-bārĭs,* thou wast } being advised	mŏnē-bāmĭnī, ye were } being advised
mŏnē-bātŭr, he was	mŏnē-bantŭr, they were

Perfect Tense (*Sup. Stem*).

mŏnĭt-ŭs sum, I was †	mŏnĭt-ī sŭmŭs, we were	
mŏnĭt-ŭs ĕs, thou wast } advised	mŏnĭt-ī estĭs, ye were } advised
mŏnĭt-ŭs est, he was	mŏnĭt-ī sunt, they were

† or, I have been, thou hast been, &c.

Future Perfect Tense (*Sup. Stem*).

mŏnĭt-ŭs ĕrō, I shall	mŏnĭt-ī ĕrĭmŭs, we shall	
mŏnĭt-ŭs ĕrĭs,thou wilt } have been advised	mŏnĭt-ī ĕrĭtĭs, ye will } have been advised
mŏnĭt-ŭs ĕrĭt, he will	mŏnĭt-ī ĕrunt, they will

Pluperfect Tense (*Sup. Stem*).

mŏnĭt-ŭs ĕram, I had	mŏnĭt-ī ĕrāmŭs, we had	
mŏnĭt-ŭs ĕrās,thou hadst } been advised	mŏnĭt-ī ĕrātĭs, ye had } been advised
mŏnĭt-ŭs ĕrăt, he had	mŏnĭt-ī ĕrant, they had

* -is or -e.

‡ *Note.*—The Tense-endings are the same as in Amor, except in the Present

34 (B). 1. Conjugate like Moneor the Passive of :—

1. **Terreo.**	2. **Doceo.**	3. **Teneo.**
4. **Timeo.***	5. **Video.**	6. **Jubeo.**

2. Give all the 3rd Persons—(1) Singular, and (2) Plural, with the English.

---

34 (C). 1. Timidus miles errebitur.
2. Potentes domini timentur.
3. Felices pueri docti sunt.
4. Pulchrae naves visae erant.
5. Mali servi moniti erunt.
6. Mons a Tito tenebatur.

1. Caesar will be feared.
2. The camp had been held.
3. The swift horses have been frightened.
4. Immense forces are seen.
5. The good children were being taught by the master.
6. The son-in-law is ordered by the father-in-law.

---

34 (D). 1. Castra Caesaris firmo praesidio tenebuntur.
2. Moenia Romae a ducibus Gallorum visa sunt.
3. Titus ab omnibus hostibus timebatur.
4. Acies ingens specie pugnae territa erat.
5. Tristis puer a magistro prudenti monitus erit.
6. Pulchra soror a fratre docebitur.

1. The cruel consul is feared by the hostages.
2. Your sisters were frightened by the teeth of the fierce animals.
3. The bridges had been held by the brave citizens.
4. The harbours of Kent will be seen by the sailors or the enemy.
5. The man had been advised by the faithful friend.
6. The children of the judge will have been taught by Galba.

---

* Verbs which have no Supine are wanting in Supine Stem Tenses.

35 (A).   PASSIVE VOICE.
rĕg-ŏr, rĕg-ī, rect-ŭs, I am ruled.
Indicative Mood.‡
Present Tense (*Pres. Stem*).

SINGULAR.	PLURAL.
rĕg-ŏr, I am ruled	rĕg-īmŭr, we are ruled
rĕg-ĕrĭs,* thou art ruled	rĕg-īmĭnī, ye are ruled
rĕg-ĭtŭr, he is ruled	rĕg-untŭr, they are ruled

Future Simple Tense (*Pres. Stem*).

rĕg-ăr, I shall be	} ruled	rĕg-ēmŭr, we shall be } ruled
rĕg-ērĭs,* thou wilt be		rĕg-ēmĭnī, ye will be
rĕg-ētŭr, he will be		rĕg-entŭr, they will be

Imperfect Tense (*Pres. Stem*, with ē).

rĕg-ē-băr, I was	} being ruled	rĕg-ē-bāmŭr, we were } being ruled
rĕg-ē-bārĭs,* thou wast		rĕg-ē-bāmĭnī, ye were
rĕg-ē-bātŭr, he was		rĕg-ē-bantŭr, they were

Perfect Tense (*Sup. Stem*).

rect-ŭs sum, I was†	} ruled	rect-ī sŭmŭs, we were } ruled
rect-ŭs ĕs, thou wast		rect-ī estĭs, ye were
rect-ŭs est, he was		rect-ī sunt, they were

† or, I have been, thou hast been, &c.

Future Perfect Tense (*Sup. Stem*).

rect-ŭs ĕrŏ, I shall	} have been ruled	rect-ī ĕrĭmŭs, we shall } have been ruled
rect-ŭs ĕrĭs, thou wilt		rect-ī ĕrĭtĭs, ye will
rect-ŭs ĕrĭt, he will		rect-ī ĕrunt, they will

Pluperfect Tense (*Sup. Stem*).

rect-ŭs ĕram, I had	} been ruled	rect-ī ĕrāmŭs, we had } been ruled
rect-ŭs ĕrās, thou hadst		rect-ī ĕrātĭs, ye had
rect-ŭs ĕrăt, he had		rect-ī ĕrant, they had

* -ĭs or -ė.

‡ *Note.*—The Tense-endings are the same as in Moneor, except in the Present and Future

35 (B). 1. Conjugate like Regor the Passive of:—

   1. **Duco.**   2. **Cingo.**   3. **Frango.**

   4. **Vinco.**   5. **Mitto.**   6. **Defendo.**

2. Give all the 3rd Persons—(1) Singular, and (2) Plural, with the English.

---

35 (C). 1. Mons ab hostibus cingebatur.

2. Equitatus omnis a Tito mittitur.

3. Castra nostra defensa sunt.

4. Sagitta a servo frangetur.

5. Copiae ingentes a Caesare ductae erant.

6. Galli a consulibus victi erunt.

1. The swifter chariot had been broken.

2. The town is surrounded by a broad river.

3. The gates were being defended by the cavalry.

4. Your armies will be conquered by the Cimbri.

5. The heavy waggons will have been drawn.

6. A lieutenant has been sent by the leader.

---

35 (D). 1. Roma moenibus altis cincta erat.

2. Soror militis telis Titi defendetur.

3. Galli a Caesare magna pernicie victi sunt.

4. Carri Senonum ab equis celerrimis ducebantur.

5. Magnae naves a civibus missae erant.

6. Spes Gallorum adventu Caesaris fractae erunt.

1. The camp of Caesar had been surrounded by the Gauls.

2. Your harbours had been defended with swift ships.

3. The armies (in line) of the enemy (*pl.*) will have been conquered by our soldiers.

4. The gates of the strongest cities will be broken by hard blows.

5. An army of faithful citizens is led by the consul.

6. Hostages were being sent by the fierce Cimbri.

36 (A). PASSIVE VOICE.
aud-ĭŏr, audī-rī, audīt-ŭs, I am heard.
Indicative Mood.‡
Present Tense (*Clipt Stem*).

SINGULAR.	PLURAL.
aud-ĭŏr, I am heard	aud-īmŭr, we are heard
aud-īrĭs,* thou art heard	aud-īmĭnī, ye are heard
aud-ītŭr, he is heard	aud-ĭuntŭr, they are heard

Future Simple Tense (*Pres. Stem*).

audĭ-ăr, I shall be	⎞	audĭ-ēmŭr, we shall be	⎞
audĭ-ērĭs,* thou wilt be	⎬ heard	audĭ-ēmĭnī, ye will be	⎬ heard
audĭ-ētŭr, he will be	⎠	audĭ-entŭr, they will be	⎠

Imperfect Tense (*Pres. Stem* with ē).

audĭ-ē-băr, I was	⎞	audĭ-ē-bāmŭr, we were	⎞
audĭ-ē-bārĭs,* thou wast	⎬ being heard	audĭ-ē-bāmĭnī, ye were	⎬ being heard
audĭ-ē-bātŭr, he was	⎠	audĭ-ē-bantŭr, they were	⎠

Perfect Tense (*Sup. Stem*).

audīt-ŭs sum, I was†	⎞	audīt-ī sŭmŭs, we were	⎞
audīt-ŭs ĕs, thou wast	⎬ heard	audīt-ī estĭs, ye were	⎬ heard
audīt-ŭs est, he was	⎠	audīt-ī sunt, they were	⎠

† or, I have been, thou hast been, &c.

Future Perfect Tense (*Sup. Stem*).

audīt-ŭs ĕrō, I shall	⎞	audīt-ī ĕrĭmŭs, we shall	⎞
audīt-ŭs ĕrĭs, thou wilt	⎬ have been heard	audīt-ī ĕrĭtĭs, ye will	⎬ have been heard
audīt-ŭs ĕrĭt, he will	⎠	audīt-ī ĕrunt, they will	⎠

Pluperfect Tense (*Sup. Stem*).

audīt-ŭs ĕram, I had	⎞	audīt-ī ĕrāmŭs, we had	⎞
audīt-ŭs ĕrās, thou hadst	⎬ been heard	audīt-ī ĕrātĭs, ye had	⎬ been heard
audīt-ŭs ĕrăt, he had	⎠	audīt-ī ĕrant, they had	⎠

* -is or -e.

‡ *Note.*—The Tense-endings are the same as in *Regor,* except in the Present.

36 (B). 1. Conjugate like Audior the Passive of :—
1. Finio.   2. Munio.   3. Punio.
4. Custodio.   5. Impedio.   6. Aperio.
2. Give all the 3rd Persons—(1) Singular, and (2)
Plural, with the English.

---

36 (C). 1. Mali pueri a magistro punientur.
2. Moenia nostra a militibus custodiuntur.
3. Castra vestra a Caesare munita erant.
4. Servi patientiores oneribus impediebantur.
5. Bellum gravissimum finitum erit.
6. Portae ingentes a servis apertae sunt.

1. Great towns were being fortified by the Cimbri.
2. The chariots have been hindered by our cavalry.
3. A very fierce battle was finished by Caesar.
4. The hostages will be guarded by prudent leaders.
5. The timid soldier had been punished by the
6. The small book will be opened.   [lieutenant.

---

36 (D). 1. Urbs nostra altissimis turribus munietur.
2. Oves domini a parvo puero custoditae erant.
3. Liberi civium innocentium a consule puniebantur.
4. Portae urbis a malo cive hostibus aperiuntur.
5. Adventus hostium nostrorum flumine latissime
    impeditur.
6. Vox ducis clarissimi a militibus audita erit.

1. The citadel of Rome was fortified with stronger
    ramparts.
2. The harbour is guarded by the more faithful citizens.
3. The sick slave has been punished by the cruel lord.
4. The march of the army had been hindered by very
    frequent stones.
5. The gate will have been opened by the consuls.
6. The names of the fairest cities will be heard by the
    leader.

37 (A).　　　Indicative Mood.

Pres. Stem.	Present Tense (*am*).					
1. Am- ŏr	ārĭs*	ātŭr	āmŭr	āmĭnī	antŭr	I am loved
2. Mŏn-ĕŏr	ērĭs	ētŭr	ēmŭr	ēmĭnī	entŭr	I am advised
3. Rĕg- ŏr	ĕrĭs	ĭtŭr	ĭmŭr	ĭmĭnī	untŭr	I am ruled
4. Aud- ĭŏr	ĭrĭs	ītŭr	īmŭr	īmĭnī	ĭuntŭr	I am heard

Pres. Stem.	Future Simple Tense (*shall or will be*).			
1. Amā-	bŏr bĕrĭs(ĕ)	3. Rĕg-	ăr,　I shall be ērĭs(ĕ),thou wilt be	1. loved
2. Mŏnē-	bĭtŭr bĭmŭr bĭmĭnī buntŭr	4. Audĭ-	ētŭr,　he will be ēmŭr,　we shall be ēmĭnī, ye will be entŭr, they will be	2. advised 3. ruled 4. heard

Pres. Stem.	Imperfect Tense (*was being*).		
1. Amā-	băr	I was being	1. loved
	barĭs(ĕ)	thou wast being	
2. Mŏnē-	bātŭr	he was being	2. advised
	bāmŭr	we were being	
3. Rĕg-ē-	bāmĭnī	ye were being	3. ruled
4. Audĭ-ē-	bantŭr	they were being	4. heard

Sup. Stem.	Perfect.		Fut. Perf.		Pluperfect.		
1. Amāt-	ŭs sum†	&c.	ŭs ĕrō	&c.	ŭs ĕram	&c.	1. loved
2. Mŏnĭt-	ŭs ĕs ŭs est	I was,	ŭs ĕrĭs ŭs ĕrĭt	have been,	ŭs ĕrās ŭs ĕrăt	had been,	2. advised
3. Rect-	ī sŭmŭs ī estĭs	I have been,	ī ĕrĭmŭs ī ĕrĭtĭs	I shall have been,	īĕrāmŭs ī ĕrātĭs	I had been,	3. ruled
4 Audīt-	ī sunt		ī ĕrunt		ī ĕrant		4. heard

* -ĭs or e.　† Fui is sometimes used for sum : fuero for ero ; fueram for eram.

37 (B). Repeat and Conjugate the Indicative Passive of any Verbs in B (24—27).

---

37 (C). 1. Patientissimi pueri a magistro laudabantur.
2. Currus celcriores a duce videntur.
3. Agri feracissimi ab hostibus vastati erant. ▮
4. Exercitus magnus a Tito ducetur.
5. Servi miserrimi a domino puniti erunt.
6. Triste bellum a Caesare finitum est.

1. The little sister will have been taught by the brother.
2. The heaviest burdens will be carried by the black slaves.
3. A harder dart was being broken by the strong man.
4. More beautiful books have been sent by the father-in-law.
5. The great harbour is surrounded by the swiftest ships.
6. The firmest citadels had been attacked by the fierce Gauls.

---

37 (D). 1. Victoria Caesaris civibus felicissimis nuntiatur.
2. Urbs a consule moenibus altioribus munietur.
3. Legatus a senatu Caesari missus erat.
4. Ictus lapidum magnorum a militibus timebantur.
5. Dux Senonum telo velociore vulneratus est.
6. Naves celerrimae parvis funibus tentae erunt.

1. The camp of the Senones was being guarded by a firm garrison.
2. The timid soldiers are frightened by the voice of Galba.
3. The march of the Cimbri will be hindered by a very deep river.
4. The gates of the fair city had been opened by the sad citizens.
5. The town will have been defended with a very high wall.
6. The forces of the Gauls have been conquered by the attack of our chariots.

38 (A).   Conjunctive Mood.

Clipt. Stem.	Pres. Stem.	Present Tense (*may be*).	
1. Am-ĕr	2. Mŏnĕ-	ăr, I may be	1. loved
Am-ērĭs(ĕ)		ārĭs(ĕ), thou mayst be	
Am-ētŭr		ātŭr, he may be	2. advised
Am-ēmŭr	3. Rĕg-	āmŭr, we may be	
Am-ēmĭnī		āmĭnī, ye may be	3. ruled
Am-entŭr	4. Audĭ-	antŭr, they may be	4. heard

Pres. Stem.	Imperfect Tense (*might* or *should be*).	
1. Amā-	rĕr, I might be	1. loved
2. Mŏnē-	rērĭs(ĕ), thou mightst be	
	rētŭr, he might be	2. advised
3. Rĕg-ĕ-	rēmŭr, we might be	
	rēmĭnī, ye might be	3. ruled
4. Audĭ-	rentŭr, they might be	4. heard

Sup. Stem.	Perfect Tense (*may have been*).	
1. Amāt-	ŭs sim,* I may have been	1. loved
2. Mŏnĭt-	ŭs sīs, thou mayst have been	
	ŭs sĭt, he may have been	2. advised
3. Rect-	ī sīmŭs, we may have been	3. ruled
4. Audĭt-	ī sītĭs, ye may have been	
	ī sint, they may have been	4. heard

Sup. Stem.	Pluperfect Tense (*should have been*).	
1. Amāt-	ŭs essem,† I should have been	1. loved
2. Mŏnĭt-	ŭs essēs, thou wouldst have been	
	ŭs essĕt, he would have been	2. advised
3. Rect-	ī essēmŭs, we should have been	3. ruled
4. Audĭt-	ī essētĭs, ye would have been	
	ī essent, they would have been	4. heard

* or, fuerim, &c.   † or, fuissem, &c.

38 (B). 1. Say the Conjunctive Passive of:—

1. **Laudo.**   2. **Terreo.**   3. **Cingo**
4. **Vinco.**   5. **Punio.**   6. **Do.**

2. Give all the 3rd Persons—(1) Singular, and (2) Plural, with the English.

---

38 (C). 1. Hostes pugnabunt, ne vincantur.
2. Cives timebant, ne vincerentur.
3. Portae claudentur, ne urbs oppugnetur.
4. Acies instructa est, ut oppidum cingatur.
5. Mali pueri puniti essent.
6. Timent ne naves fractae sint.

1. Soldiers fight, that they may be praised.
2. The army attacked the town, that it might be praised by the leader.
3. The cavalry will be sent, lest the camp may be attacked.
4. The mountain was being held, that Caesar might be hindered.
5. The gates have been shut, lest the citizens may be frightened.
6. The faithful slave would have been sent.

---

38 (D). 1. Milites a duce laudabuntur, ne vincatur.
2. Equitatus a Tito missus erat, ut agri nostri vastarentur.
3. Cives timebant, ne Roma a Gallis cingeretur.
4. Muri praesidio tenebuntur, ne urbs oppugnetur
5. Scuta parva militibus nostris data essent.
6. Galli timent, ne obsides a Caesare occisi sint.

1. A lieutenant was sent, that the victory might be announced to the senate.
2. Soldiers will come, that the bridge may be guarded.
3. Galba had been sent, that the army might be drawn up.
4. The timid boy fears, lest he may be punished by the master.
5. The Senones gave hostages to Caesar, lest the gates might be broken.   [praised.
6. Great wars have been waged, that leaders may be

39 (A).   Imperative Mood (*Clipt Stem*).

1. Am-	Present Tense.	1. loved
	ārĕ, be thou	
	āmĭnī, be ye	
	Future Tense.	
	ātŏr, thou must be	
	ātŏr, he must be	
	antŏr, they must be	
2. Mŏn-	Present Tense.	2. advised
	ērĕ, be thou	
	ēmĭnī, be ye	
	Future Tense.	
	ētŏr, thou must be	
	ētŏr, he must be	
	entŏr, they must be	
3. Rĕg-	Present Tense.	3. ruled
	ĕrĕ, be thou	
	ĭmĭnī, be ye	
	Future Tense.	
	ĭtŏr, thou must be	
	ĭtŏr, he must be	
	untŏr, they must be	
4. Aud-	Present Tense.	4. heard
	īrĕ, be thou	
	īmĭnī, be ye	
	Future Tense.	
	ītŏr, thou must be	
	ītŏr, he must be	
	ĭuntŏr, they must be	

39 (B). 1. Say the Imperative Passive of :—

1. **Laudo.**	2. **Doceo.**	3. **Claudo.**
4. **Frango.**	5. **Punio.**	6. **Custodio.**

---

39 (C). 1. Monemini, amici.
2. Vir fortis laudator.
3. Portae omnes clauduntor.
4. Bellum tristissimum finitor.
5. Onera gravia a servis portantor.
6. Moenia alta a civibus custodiuntor.

1. O Caesar, be thou praised.
2. Bad boys must be punished.
3. Little Titus must be carried by a slave.
4. Our city must be fortified with towers.
5. The swift arrow must be broken by the soldier.
6. O boys, be ye taught by the master.

---

39 (D). 1. Legatus mittitor, ut victoria recens civibus nuntietur.
2. Monere, Tite, ab amico prudenti.
3. Scuta militibus dantor, ne vulnerentur.
4. Bella geruntor, ne agri vastentur.
5. Oppidum vestrum altioribus muris cingitor.
6. Acies instruuntor, ne urbs ab hostibus cingatur.

1. The voice of the master must be heard by the boys.
2. The victories of Caesar must be announced to the wretched citizen.
3. Be ye advised, lest ye may be punished.
4. The sacred citadel must be guarded, lest it may be attacked by the Gauls.
5. O famous leader, be thou loved by all the soldiers.
5. Our harbours must be defended with very swift ships.

40 (A).　　**VERB INFINITE.**
Infinitive Mood.

Pres. Stem.	Present and Imperfect.	
	1. Amā-**rī**,　to be loved	
	2. Mŏnē-**rī**,　to be advised	
	3. Rĕg-**ī**,　　to be ruled	
	4. Audī-**rī**,　to be heard	

Sup. Stem.	Perfect and Pluperfect.	
1. Amāt-	**ŭs* essĕ,†** to have been	1. loved
2. Mŏnĭt-		2. advised
3. Rect-	* like Bonus.　　† or, fuisse.	3. ruled
4. Audīt-		4. heard

Sup. Stem.	Future.	
1. Amāt-		1. loved
2. Mŏnĭt-	**um īrī, to be about to be**	2. advised
3. Rect-		3. ruled
4. Audīt-		4. heard

Participles.

Sup. Stem.	Perfect (like Bonus).	
1. Amāt-		1. loved
2. Mŏnĭt-	**ŭs, ă, um,** { being, or	2. advised
3. Rect-	{ having been	3. ruled
4. Audīt-		4. heard

Clipt Stem.	Gerundive (like Bonus).	
1. Am-and-		1. loved
2. Mŏn-end-	**ŭs, ă, um, meet to be**	2. advised
3. Rĕg-end-		3. ruled
4. Aud-ĭend-		4. heard

40 (B). Say the Infinitive Passive of any Verbs in B (24—31), omitting Venio.

40 (C). 1. Caesar pontem muniri jubet.
2. Bellum tristissimum paratum esset.
3. Consul absens timet, ne exercitus victus sit.
4. Signum datum est, ut moenia oppugnarentur.
5. Urbs munitor, ne cives terreantur.
6. Bellum magnum a Gallis gestum est.

1. All boys love to be praised.
2. The consuls fought, lest Rome might be conquered.
3. The gates must be shut, that the city may be defended. [praised.
4. Bad slaves will be punished : good (slaves) will be
5. The timid sisters fear, lest the brother may have been killed. [patient animals.
6. Very heavy burdens will have been carried by the

40 (D). 1. Caesar castra altiore muro muniri jussit.
2. Scuta militibus data sunt, ne vulnerentur.
3. Urbs muro cingētur, ne ab hostibus vastetur.
4. Carri mittuntor, ut lapides portent.
5. Victoria Caesaris a legato civibus nuntiata erat.
6. Caesar montem ab equitatu teneri jubebit, ne iter ab hostibus impediatur.

1. The absent consul had ordered the gates of the citadel to be shut. [broken.
2. The gates had been opened, lest they might be
3. Good books are given by the masters, that the boys may be taught.
4. A double line-of-battle was drawn up, that the city might be guarded.
5. An immense army will be led by Titus, that the town may be attacked.
6· The camp of the Cimbri was seen by our soldiers.

41 (A). Căp-ĭ-ŏ, căp-ĕrĕ, cēp-ī, capt-um, I take, capture.

Note.—The Present Stem is Clipt before i, short ĕr, and final ĕ.

ACTIVE VOICE.
Clipt Stem (**Căp-**) Tenses.

Ind. Pres.	Conj. Imperf.	Imper. Pres.	Infin. Pres.
Căp-ĭŏ	Căp-ĕ-rem	Căp-ĕ	Căp-ĕrĕ
ĭs	ĕ-rēs	ĭtĕ	
ĭt	ĕ-rĕt	(*Future*)	
ĭmŭs	ĕ-rēmŭs	Căp-ĭtō	
ĭtĭs	ĕ-rētĭs	ĭtōtĕ	
ĭunt	ĕ-rent	ĭunto	

Present Stem (**Căpĭ-**) Tenses.

Ind. Fut. Sim.	Ind. Imperf.	Conj. Pres.	Part. Pres.
Căpĭ-am	Căpĭ-ē-bam	Căpĭ-am	Căpĭ-ens

Gerund. Căpĭ-end-um, -ī, -ō.

PASSIVE VOICE.
Clipt Stem (**Căp-**) Tenses.

Indic. Pres.	Conj. Imperf.	Imper. Pres.	Infin. Pres.
Căp-ĭŏr	Căp-ĕ-rĕr	Căp-ĕrĕ	Căp-ī
ĕrĭs	ĕ-rērĭs	ĭmĭnĭ	
ĭtŭr	ĕ-rētŭr	(*Future*)	
ĭmŭr	ĕ-rēmŭr	Căp-ĭtŏr	
ĭmĭnī	ĕ rēmĭnī	ĭtŏr	
ĭuntŭr	ĕ rentŭr	ĭuntor	

Present Stem (**Căpĭ-**) Tenses.

Ind. Fut. Sim.	Ind. Imperf.	Conj. Pres.	Gerundive.
Căpĭ-ăr	Căpĭ-ē-băr	Căpĭ-ăr	Căpĭ-end ŭs

The Perfect-stem Tenses are like **Rego**.

41 (B). 1. Learn the Principal Parts (p. 45) of
    1. **Jacio.**   2. **Facio.**   3. **Conficio.**
    4. **Interficio.** 5. **Accipio.**   6. **Fugio.**
  2. Find their Stems, and conjugate them like Capio.*
  3. Give all the 3rd Persons—(1) Singular, and
(2) Plural, of both Voices, with the English.

---

41 (C). 1. Hostes tela velocia jaciebant.
2. Galli signiferum nostrum interficiunt.
3. Hostis venit, ut impetum faciat.
4. Animal patiens vulnus gravius acceperat.
5 Iter longissimum a Caesare confectum est.
6. Equi fugient, ne ictūs accipiant.

1. The Cimbri prepare to make a long journey.
2. The consuls are killed by the Gauls.
3. The Gauls were fleeing, lest they might be captured.
4. A very heavy wound was received by Galba.
5. Caesar will finish the great war.
6. Great stones are thrown by the enemies.

---

41 (D). 1. Cives fugiunt, ne a militibus interficiantur.
2. Fugite, cives, ne vulnera accipiatis.
3. Pacem faciunt, ne urbs capiatur.
4. Hostes lapides jaciunt, ut nostros milites vulnerent.
5. Milites impetum fecerunt, ut oppidum caperent.
6. Dux Gallorum obsides interficere constituit.

1. The citizens were holding the walls, that they might
   cast stones.
2. The children of the citizens had been killed with
   arrows.
3. A strong town of Kent will be captured by the ships
   of the enemy.   [he may flee.
4. The leader has ordered the hostage to be killed, lest
5. A firm peace was made by our consul.
6. The happy boy has received a most beautiful book
   from the master.

---

* *Note.*—**Fugio** has no Passive Voice; and the Present-stem Tenses of
the Passive of **Facio** are irregular, and will be given at page 97.

J

42 (**A**). Deponent Verbs are chiefly *Passive* in *form*, but *Active* in *meaning*.

They have also of the Active form, the Infinitive Future, the Gerund, Supines and Participles.

DEPONENT VERBS.

Hort-ŏr, hortā-rī, hortāt-ŭs, I exhort.

Indicative Mood.		
Present	Hort- ŏr	I exhort
Fut. Sim.	Hortā- bŏr	I shall exhort
Imperf.	Hortā- băr	I was exhorting
Perfect	Hortāt- ŭs sum	I have exhorted
Fut. Perf.	Hortāt- ŭs ĕrō	I shall have exhorted
Pluperf.	Hortāt- ŭs ĕram	I had exhorted

Conjunctive Mood.		
Present	Hort- ĕr	I may exhort
Imperf	Hortā- rĕr	I might exhort
Perfect	Hortāt- ŭs sim	I may have exhorted
Pluperf.	Hortāt- ŭs essem	I should have exhorted

Imperative Mood.		
Present	Hortā- rĕ	exhort thou
Future	Hortā- tŏr	he must exhort

Infinitive Mood.		
Pres. & Imperf.	Hortā- rī	to exhort
Perf. & Pluper.	Hortāt-ŭs essĕ	to have exhorted
*Future**	Hortāt-ūrŭs essĕ	to be about to exhort

* *Note* – There is no Future Infinitive of the Passive form.

Gerund.	
Hort-and-um, -i, -ŏ, -ŏ	exhorting, of exhorting, &c.

Supines.	
Hortāt-um, to exhort	Hortāt-ū, to be exhorted

Participles.		
Present	Hort-ans	exhorting
Future	Hortāt-ūrŭs	about to exhort
Perfect	Hortāt-ŭs	having exhorted
Gerundive°	Hort-and-ŭs	(meet) to be exhorted

* *Note.*—Intransitive Deponents have no Gerundive Participle.

42 (B). Deponent Verbs.

1. Learn the Principal Parts of :—

   1. **Cōn-ŏr**, -ārī, ātŭs, (1) I endeavour, attempt.
   2. **Mīr-ŏr**, -ārī, -ātŭs, (1) I admire, wonder at.
   3. **Vĕr-ĕŏr**, -ērī, -ĭtŭs, (2) I fear.
   4. **Sĕqŭ-ŏr**, -ī, sĕcūt-ŭs, (3) I follow, pursue.
   5. **Prōfĭcīsc-ŏr**, -ī, prŏfect-ŭs, (3) I set out, advance.
   6. **Adŏr-ĭŏr**, -irī, ădort-ŭs, (4) I attack (suddenly)

2. Find their Stems, and conjugate them like the Passive Voice of their respective Conjugations, giving the English as in Hortoᵣ.

3. Give all the 3rd Persons (1) Singular, and (2) Plural, of the Finite Verb, with the English.

4. Give all their parts which are like the Active Voice.

5. Why has *proficiscor* no Gerundive Participle?

42 (C). 1. Dux milites hortabitur, ut pugnent.
2. Tenera soror periculum magnum verita est.
3. Pueri equos pulcherrimos mirantur.
4. Legatus noster profectus esset.
5. Sequimini ducem vestrum, milites.
6. Cimbri iter facere conantur.

1. The lord was admiring the fruitful fields.
2. The Gauls will attack our camp.
3. The timid citizens feared, lest they might be killed.
4. The wretched hostages were endeavouring to flee.
5. The animals followed the army, lest they might be wounded.
6. Caesar orders the army to set out.

---

42 (D). 1. Dux proficiscitur, exercitus omnis sequitur.
2. Hostes agmen lapidibus impedire conati sunt.
3. Titus verebatur, ne copiae hostium impetum facerent.
4. Puer mare magnum mirabitur.
5. Galba equitatum misit, ut agmen Gallorum sequeretur.
6. Moenia hostium adoriuntor.

1. The workman admired the long horns of the animals.
2. The enemy would have fled, our soldiers would have pursued.
3. The citizens were fearing, lest the Gauls might attack the gates of the city.
4. Caesar will set out, that he may conquer the Cimbri.
5. The sick soldiers had endeavoured to pursue the enemy.
6. Exhort thou the sailors, that they may defend the harbour.

Personal Pronouns.

43 (A). First Person.

	SINGULAR.		PLURAL.	
Nom.	**Egŏ**	I	**Nōs**	we
Acc.	**Mē**	me	**Nōs**	us
Gen.	**Mĕī**	of me	**Nostr-um** or **ī**	of us
Dat.	**Mĭhi**	to or for me	**Nōbīs**	to or for us
Abl.	**Mē**	(with) me	**Nōbīs**	(with) us

Second Person.

N. V.	**Tŭ**	thou, O thou	**Vōs**	ye or you
Acc.	**Tē**	thee	**Vōs**	you
Gen.	**Tŭī**	of thee	**Vestr-um** or **ī**	of you
Dat.	**Tĭbi**	to or for thee	**Vōbīs**	to or for you
Abl.	**Tē**	(with) thee	**Vōbīs**	(with) you

Reflexive* (Third Person).
Singular and Plural alike.

Nom.	wanting.	
Acc.	**Sē (sese),**	himself, herself, itself, themselves.
Gen.	**Sŭī**	of himself, &c.
Dat.	**Sĭbi**	to or for himself, &c.
Abl.	**Sē (sēsē)**	(with) himself, &c.

---

43 (B). Possessive Pronouns (like Bonus).

Mĕ-ŭs, ă, ŭm, my, mine (Voc. Masc. Sing. **mī**).
Tŭ-ŭs, ă, ŭm, thy, thine (no Voc.).
Sŭ-ŭs, ă, ŭm, his, her, its, their (own) (no Voc.).

Like Niger. .

Nostĕr, our, ours ; **Vestĕr,** your, yours (see p. 26).

(see p. 26)

Decline together :—

1. Meus frater.	4. Spes omnis nostra.
2. Tua soror.	5. Vestra moenia firma.
3. Suum caput.	6. Sua manus dextra.

Note.—Se and Suus always refer to the Subject of the sentence.

---

* The oblique Cases of **Ego** and **Tu** are used reflexively for **myself, thyself,** &c.

43 (C). 1. Ego* te miror, tu me terres.
2. Vos hortabimur, pueri, ut nos audiatis.
3. Tu sororem meam laudavisti.
4. Nos pericula maris timebamus.
5. Mi frater, audi vocem magistri.
6. Vos me interficere conati estis.

1. I shall praise thee, thou wilt punish me.
2. We make war, that ye may have peace.
3. My sisters will be very happy, thine will be very wretched.
4. All our (men) kill themselves, lest they may be captured.
5. The bad slave killed his (own) lord.
6. We will lead you, ye will follow us.

---

43 (D). 1. Ego a te laudabor, tu a me punieris.
2. Magister a nobis omnibus amatus erit.
3. Vos me gladiis vestris vulneravistis.
4. Ego tibi pacem dedi, tu mihi ictus dedisti.
5. Titus ducem Gallorum manu suâ occidit.
6. Res magnae a nobis confectae sunt.

1. The citizens were defending themselves with high walls.
2. The standard-bearer announced the thing to me.
3. The consul frightens the citizens with his voice.
4. The names of our leaders are very famous.
5. We shall be praised by you, you will be defended by us.
6. A small victory will afford great hope to us all.

* See note, 18 (B).

44 (A).   1. **Hic,** this (near me).

	SINGULAR.			PLURAL.		
Nom.	Hīc	haec	hōc	Hī	hae	haec
Acc.	Hunc	hanc	hōc	Hōs	hās	haec
Gen.		Hūjŭs		Hōrum	hārum	hōrum
Dat.		Huic		Hīs		
Abl.	Hōc	hāc	hōc	Hīs		

2. **Ille,** that (yonder).

Nom.	Illĕ	illă	illŭd	Illī	illae	illă
Acc.	Illum	illam	illŭd	Illōs	illās	illă
Gen.		Illiŭs		Illōrum	illārum	illōrum
Dat.		Illī		Illīs		
Abl.	Illō	illā	illō	Illis		

3. **Is,*** he, she, it, that, they.

Nom.	Is	ĕă	ĭd	Iī	ĕae	ĕă
Acc.	Eum	ĕam	ĭd	Eōs	ĕās	ĕă
Gen.		Ejus		Eōrum	ĕārum	ĕōrum
Dat.		Eī		Iīs or ĕīs		
Abl.	Eō	ĕā	ĕō	Iīs or ĕīs		

4. **Idem,** same.

Nom.	Idem	ĕădem	ĭdem	Iīdem	ĕaedem	ĕădem
Acc.	Eundem	ĕandem	ĭdem	Eōsdem	ĕasdem	ĕădem
Gen.		Ejusdem		Eōrundem	ĕārundem	ĕōrun-
Dat.		Eīdem		Iisdem or ĕisdem		[dem
Abl.	Eōdem	ĕădem	ĕōdem	Iisdem or ĕisdem		

44 (B). Learn and decline like Ille :—

Iste, that (near you).

Ipse, self, myself, thyself, &c.(Sing. Neut. Nom. Acc. **ipsum**).

Decline together :—

1. Ego ipse.   2. Idem ille dux.   3. Ista tua soror.
4. Haec dies.   5. Illud magnum onus.   6. Idem ingens rete.

---

* *Note.*—**Hic, iste, ille,** may all be translated by **he. she, it, they,** when used without a Noun. **Is** refers to some person or thing mentioned in the clause preceding or following—as **Titum** amo, **eum** laudabo.

44 (C). *Note.*—Adjectives are used as Nouns, the words **man, thing,** &c., being understood, as **fortis**, *a* (or *the*) *brave man,* **hoc**, *this thing.*

1. Hic miles fortis est, ille* timidus.
2. Haec animalia illa onera portabunt.
3. Caesar id oppidum oppugnare parabat.
4. Senones eandem rem facere constituerunt.
5. Isti servi fideles sunt, dominus eos laudabit.
6. Te ipsum laudavisti, ego te puniveram.

1. This river is very deep, that (one) is very broad.
2. These great dangers will frighten Galba himself.
3. The same armies conquered those cities.
4. Those boys (yonder) are very cruel, I will punish
5. We admire ourselves.†   [them.
6. Caesar orders them to be killed.

---

44 (D). 1. Nomen illius ducis clarissimum erat.
2. Portae harum urbium fractae sunt.
3. Hi telis, illi lapidibus se defendere conantur.
4. Sorores ejus pueri felicissimae sunt.
5. His sagittas, illis scuta dabunt.
6. Gallos timeo, ab iis interficiar.

1. I will kill this man with this sword.
2. Titus is a good boy, I will give that book to him.
3. These (things) were announced to Caesar by the same hostage.
4. He wounded himself with his own sword.
5. We have heard the names of those brave men.
6. Caesar appointed a day for that thing.

---

* Supply 'miles' and 'est' from the first clause. Avoid using the same word twice in a Latin sentence. † use ego ipse.

45 (A). Qui, who, which, what.

| | SINGULAR. | | | PLURAL. | |
	M.	F.	N.	M.	F.	N.
Nom.	Quī	quae	quŏd	Quī	quae	quae
Acc.	Quem	quam	quŏd	Quŏs	quās	quae
Gen.		Cūjŭs		Quōrum	quārum	quōrum
Dat.		Cui			Quíbŭs or quīs	
Abl.	Quŏ	quă	quŏ		Quíbŭs or quīs	

Interrogative.

Quis or **Qui**, who? what?

	SINGULAR.		
Nom.	Quĭs (quĭs)	quĭd
Acc.	Quem	quam	quĭd
	&c., like Qui.	

Indefinite.

Quis or **Qui**, any, any one.

	SINGULAR.		
	Quĭs	quă	quĭd
	Quem	quam	quĭd
	&c., like Qui,	
	but Pl. Neut. Nom. Acc. quae or quă.	

The Interrogative and Indefinite Qui is used when joined to a Noun, and is declined like the Relative.

---

45 (B). *Rule 8.*—The Relative agrees with its Antecedent in Gender, Number, and Person, but takes its Case from its own clause, as

(1) Puer, **qui** magistrum amat, bonus est.

The boy, **who** loves the master, is good.

Explanation.—**Qui** is Masc. Sing. to agree with its Antecedent Puer, but Nom. because it is the Subject to amat.

(2) Puer, **quem** magister amat, bonus est.

The boy, **whom** the master loves, is good.

Explanation.—**Quem** is Masc. Sing. to agree with puer, as before, but it is Acc. because it is the Object to amat.

Note.—The Relative, of whatever Case, generally stands at the beginning of its clause, as in English

45 (C). 1. Magister, qui me docet, patiens est.
2. Puer, quem hic magister docet, felix est.
3. Illa soror, quae fratrem amat, laudabitur.
4. Illa soror, quam frater amat, laudata est.
5. Agmen, quod Caesar duxit, Gallos terruit.
6. Felices sunt illi, quos omnes* laudant.

1. The arrows, which the Gaul holds, are very long.
2. We admire the ships, which defend our harbours.
3. The soldiers, who wounded the consul, were killed.
4. The Cimbri feared the armies, which Caesar led.
5. The marches, which Titus made, were very long.
6. He is a brave man, who conquers himself.

---

45 (D). 1. Ii cives boni sunt, qui urbem defendunt.
2. Caesar milites laudat, a quibus hostes victi sunt.
3. Servus, cui telum datum est, fidelis est.
4. Obsides, qui fugere conabantur, a Caesare occisi sunt.
5. Quis vestrum Gallos timet?
6. Quis eum mirabitur, qui se ipsum laudat?

1. The cavalry, which Titus sent, frightened the forces of the Cimbri.
2. The leaders, to whom Caesar gave the hostages, were slain.
3. The soldiers, whose leaders are brave, will conquer.
4. The wars, which Caesar waged, were immense.
5. Who of us will fear the dangers, by which we are surrounded?
6. Whose† is this book?   Mine.

---

* See Note, 44 (C).   † say, of whom?

46 (A). (Genitive Singular -ius, Dative -i). No Vocative.

Unŭs, one, alone.			Alĭŭs, another, other, some.		
SINGULAR.			SINGULAR.		
Nom. Un-ŭs	-ă	-um	Alĭ-ŭs	-ă	-ŭd
Acc. Un-um	-am	-um	Alĭ-um	-am	-ud
Gen.	Un-īŭs*			Al-īŭs	
Dat.	Un-ī			Al-ĭī	
Abl. Un-ŏ	-ā	-ŏ	Alĭ-ŏ	-ā	-ŏ
Plural† like Bonus.			Plural like Bonus.		

Utĕr, which (of the two)?			Altĕr, the one, the other, the second.		
SINGULAR.			SINGULAR.		
Nom. Utĕr utr-ă	utr-um		Altĕr	-ă	-um
Acc. Utr-um	-am	-um	Altĕr-um	-am	-um
Gen.	Utr-īŭs			Altĕr-ĭŭs	
Dat.	Utr-ī			Altĕr-ī	
Abl. Utr-ŏ	-ă	ŏ	Altĕr-ŏ	-ā	-o
Plural like Niger.			Plural like Tener.		

Dŭŏ, two.			Trēs, three.	
Nom. Dŭ-ŏ	-ae	-ŏ	Trēs	trĭă
Acc. Dŭ-ōs or ŏ	-ās	-ŏ	Trēs	trĭă
Gen. Dŭ-ōrum	-ārum	-ōrum	Trĭum	
Dat. Dŭ-ōbŭs	-ābŭs	-ōbŭs	Trĭbŭs	
Abl. Dŭ-ōbŭs	-ābŭs	-ōbŭs	Trĭbŭs	

46 (B). Learn and decline like Unus :—Ullŭs, any ;
Nullŭs, no, none ; Sōlŭs, alone ; Tōtŭs, the whole.
Like Utĕr :—Neutĕr, neither ; Uterquĕ,‡ each, both.
Like Duo :—Ambō, both (together).
Decline together :—
1. Haec una dies. 3. Ambo consules. 5. Tres pueri.
2. Una castra. 4. Altera manus. 6. Nullum aliud iter.

* Unus has sometimes i (short) in the Genitive.
† Only used when joined to a Plural Noun, with singular meaning.
‡ Utraque, Utrumque, &c.

46 (C). 1. Hostes totam planitiem vastaverant.
2. Uter consul vulneratus est?
3. Alii capti,* alii occisi sunt.
4. Uter fortior est? quis fortissimus erat?
5. Nullum aliud iter erat.†
6. Magister alterum puerum laudabit, alterum puniet.

1. The Gauls had no other leaders.
2. Which gate (of the two) has been shut?
3. We admire Caesar alone.‡
4. They§ alone are wretched, who are bad.
5. Both the consuls have been slain.
6. Who has any hope of victory?

---

46 (D). 1. Ille vir est fortis, quem nulla pericula terrent.
2. Senatus utrique consuli exercitum credidit.
3. Caesar alteri gladium, alteri sagittam dat.
4. Nostri milites nullam spem victoriae habebant.
5. Utri nautarum retia dedisti? Neutri.
6. Duae urbes fortissimae ab uno duce captae sunt.

1. Three great wars were waged by the same leader.
2. The whole town is surrounded by a double wall.
3. With which hand was‖ the sailor holding the rope? With both.¶
4. The standard-bearer holds the standard with one hand, he defends himself with the other.
5. There were two roads, of which one was long, the other rough.
6. The consul will praise those alone, who are good citizens.

---

* Supply sunt.   + there was.   ‡ unus.   § is.
‖ 'was holding' is the Imperfect of Teneo.   ¶ supply, hands.

47 (A). 1. Prepositions which take the Accusative.

Ad, to	**Intrā**, within
Antĕ, before	**Pĕr**, through
Circum, around	**Post**, after, behind
Contrā, against, opposite to	**Proptĕr**, on account of
Extrā, outside	**Trans**, across.
Intĕr, between, among	

2. Prepositions which take the Ablative.

A, ăb, by, from	**Ex, ē**, out of, from
Cum, with, together with	**Prō**, before, for, instead of
Dē, from, concerning	**Sĭnĕ**, without

3. Prepositions which take the Accusative or Abl.

In, into, against (Acc.), in, upon, among (Abl.)
Sŭb, under, up to (Acc.), beneath (Abl.)

Note.—In and Sub take the Accusative in answer to the question **Whither?** and the Ablative in answer to the question **Where?**

---

47 (B). Learn and decline (see 11 B) :—

Arm-ă, ōrum (*n.P.*), arms	**Lĕgĭ-o, ōnĭs** (*f.*), a legion
Britann-ī, ōrum (*m.P.*), Britons	**Mult-ŭs, ă, um**, much, many
Britannĭ-ă, ae (*f.S.*), Britain	**Pars, part-ĭs** (*f.*), a part
Cassĭvĕlaun-ŭs -ī, (*m.S.*), Cassivelaunus	**Proelĭ-um, ī** (*n.*), an engagement
Fīn-ēs, ĭum (*m.P.*), borders	**Rōmān-ŭs, ă, um**, Roman
Foss-ă, ae (*f.*), a ditch	**Rex, rēg-ĭs** (*m.*), a king
Gallĭ-ă, ae (*f.S.*), Gaul	**Vall-um, ī** (*n.*), a mound (set with palisades)

Note.—Prepositions usually stand **before** the words they govern. But a Genitive may stand **between** a Preposition and its Noun, as **de Caesaris adventu**, *concerning the approach of Caesar ;* or the Preposition may stand between an Adjective and its Noun, for the sake of emphasis, as **magno cum periculo,** *with great danger.*

47 (C) 1. Caesar equitatum omnem ante se mittit.
2. Legati ex Britannia ad Caesarem venerunt.
3. Consul tres legiones trans flumen duxerat.
4. Galli copias Romanorum post se viderunt
5. Omnes milites pro castris pugnabant.
6. Cives prudentes arma secum* portabunt.

1. The Britons send another lieutenant to Caesar.
2. The Senones pitched their camp under (at the foot of) the mountain.   [Britain.
3. The ships of the Romans had been broken in
4. The citizens were throwing stones from the towers into the ditch.
5. Three soldiers were captured outside the gates.
6. Among the hostages was the sister of the king.

---

47 (D). 1. Hostes legatos ad Caesarem de pace miserunt.   [ficiscitur.
2. Titus duabus cum legionibus in Senones pro-
3. Consul milites, quos circum se habebat, se sequi jussit.
4. Romani iter per fines Cimbrorum magno cum periculo fecerunt.
5. In eo proelio magna pars hostium occisa est.
6. Dux Romanus a senatu propter victorias ipsius laudabitur.

1. Caesar prepares to set out into (for) Britain.
2. He had determined to wage war with the Britons.
3. He led a great army through the borders of Cassivelaunus.
4. After this battle the Britons send hostages to Caesar.
5. All who were captured within the walls were slain.
6. Caesar set out from† the camp without any guard.

---

* Cum is affixed to the Personal Pronouns: as mecum, with me; tecum, with thee, &c.   † use e.

48 (A). Adverbs are formed from Adjectives of the 1st and 2nd Declensions by adding ē to the Stem, and from Adjectives of the 3rd Declension by adding ĭtĕr to the Stem, as—

> pulcher, *beautiful;* pulchrē, *beautifully;* fortis, *brave;* fort-ĭtĕr, *bravely;*

but Stems ending in nt add only ĕr, as
> prudens, *prudent;* prudent-ĕr, *prudently.*

The Comparatives and Superlatives of Adverbs are formed from those of Adjectives by changing—

> Comp. ĭŏr to ĭŭs, and Sup. ŭs to ē.

Pos.	Comp.	Sup.
Adj. fort-ĭs	fort-ĭŏr	fortissĭm-ŭs.
Adv. fort-ĭtĕr	fort-ĭŭs	fortissĭm-ē.
bravely	*more or too bravely*	*most or very bravely*

Form Adverbs from the Adjectives in 17 (B) (omitting Ingens), and compare them.

Learn the following:—nōn, not; jam, now, already; sempĕr, always; nunquam, never; unquam, ever.

---

48 (B). Conjunctions are of two kinds—

1. **Co-ordinative,** which join like Cases, Moods, and Tenses, as ĕt, and; quĕ (at the end of a word), and; sĕd, but; quam, than.

2. **Sub-ordinative,** which affect Mood, as ŭt, that; nē, lest; quum, when; sĭ, if; nĭsi, unless, which commonly govern the Subjunctive. The last three give to the Subjunctive the English of the Indicative, as quum audivisset, *when he had heard.*

Rule for the Sequence of Tenses.—Primary Tenses follow Primary, Historic follow Historic—see 18 (B).

48 (C). *Rule* 9.—Two or more Singular Nominatives take a Plural Verb.

1. Caesar bellum feliciter* gessit.
2. Galba et Titus acriter† pugnaverunt.
3. Ex vallo turribusque tela jaciebant.
4. Si acrius pugnavissent, victi non essent.
5. Hostes jam velocissime fugiebant.
6. Romani obsides accipient, non dabunt.‡

1. Our (men) quickly took (up) arms.   [enemy.
2. The legion made an attack too eagerly§ upon the
3. All fought most eagerly and most bravely.
4. The consul will fortify the camp with a mound and ‖ a ditch.   [for¶ Britain.
5. When Caesar had conquered the Gauls, he set out
6. Unless you come more quickly, I will punish you.

48 (D). 1. Caesar milites hortabitur, ut fortiter pugnent.
2. Miles fortis periculo belli non gravissime terrebitur.
3. Si obsides a Cimbris Caesari dentur, cum iis pacem faciet.
4. Hostes, qui acrius sequuntur, a nostris interficiuntur.
5. Caesar et Titus a senatu Romano laudati sunt.
6. Nisi Romani fortissime pugnavissent, Britannos nunquam vicissent.

1. The consul orders the gates to be shut, lest the Gauls may attempt to take the city.
2. The Britons would have conquered the Roman legions, if they had had a better leader.
3. Unless the standard-bearer had defended himself, he would have been captured.
4. When the Britons saw the ships of the Romans, they fled very quickly.   [town.
5. When the enemy had fled, the legions captured the
6. No Roman leader ever waged wars more successfully than Caesar.

---

* Say successfully.   † sharply.   ‡ supply obsides.   § say sharply,
‖ use que.   ¶ into.

49 (A). Anomalous Verbs are irregular in some of the Tense-endings of the Present-stem forms.

1. Possum possĕ pŏtŭī —— I am able, can
2. Vŏlo vellĕ vŏlŭī —— I am willing, wish
3. Nōlo nollĕ nōlŭī —— I am unwilling
4. Mālo mallĕ mālŭī —— I am more willing, prefer
5. Fĕrō ferrĕ tŭlī lātum I bear, endure
6. Fīō fĭĕrī (factŭs sum)—— I am made or done, become
7. Eō īrĕ īvī (or īī) ĭtum I go

49 (B). **Indicative Mood.**

Present Tense.					
1. Possum*	pŏtĕs	pŏtest	possŭmŭs	pŏtestĭs	pōssunt
2. Vŏlo	vīs	vult	vŏlŭmŭs	vultĭs	vŏlunt
3. Nōlo	nonvīs	nonvult	nōlŭmŭs	nonvultĭs	nōlunt
4. Mālo	māvīs	māvult	mālŭmŭs	māvultĭs	mālunt
5. Fĕrō	fers	fert	fĕrĭmŭs	fertĭs	fĕrunt
6. Fīō	fīs	fĭt	——	——	fīunt
7. Eō	īs	ĭt	īmŭs	ĭtĭs	ĕunt

Future Simple Tense.				
1. Pŏt-ĕrō	2. Vŏl-	am	7. I-bō	
ĕrĭs	3. Nōl-	ēs	bĭs	
ĕrĭt	4. Māl-	ĕt	bĭt	
ĕrĭmŭs	5. Fĕr-	ēmŭs	bĭmŭs	
ĕrĭtĭs	6. Fī-	ētis	bĭtĭs	
ĕrunt		ent	bunt	

Imperfect Tense.				
1. Pŏt-ĕram	2. Vŏlē-	bam	7. I-bam	
ĕrās	3. Nōlē-	bās	bās	
ĕrăt	4. Mālē-	băt	băt	
ĕrāmŭs	5. Fĕrē-	bāmŭs	bāmŭs	
ĕrātĭs	6. Fīē-	bātĭs	bātĭs	
ĕrant		bant	bant	

The Perfect-stem Tenses are formed regularly.

Fio makes the Perfect-stem Tenses, Factus sum, etc., like the Passive Voice of Facio.

Conjugate like Eo:—Ex-ĕo, I go out; Rĕd-ĕo, I return; Trans-ĕo, I cross over.

———

* Like sum.

H

49 (C). 1. Britanni obsides dare volunt.

2. Romani capi nolebant, interfici ma'ebant.

3. Galli e finibus suis exibunt.

4. Proelium fit in ea planitie.   ⌈poterant.

5. Omnes naves in eundem portum venire non

6. Vir fortis omnia mala* patienter fert.

1. Ye will conquer, if ye wish.†

2. The master is unwilling to punish innocent boys.

3. The fierce Gauls will not be able to take the firm citadel.

4. A brave soldier prefers to fight (rather) than to flee.

5. Caesar will cross over into Britain with an immense army.

6. After this battle the legions returned into the camp.

---

49 (D). 1. Si pacem habere vis, bellum para.

2. Malus est ille, qui se vincere nonvult.

3. Propter flumen Galli iter facere non potuerant.

4. Hostes impetum curruum nostrorum non tulerunt.

5. Galli flumen jam transibant, quum Caesar eos adortus est.

6. Britanni servi ‡ nunquam fient.

1. Caesar conquered others, he was not able to conquer himself.

2. The citizens preferred to defend themselves (rather) than to give hostages.   [burdens.

3. A bad slave will be unwilling to carry very light

4. On account of many and great victories Caesar was made consul.

5. These soldiers, who wished to be praised, have fought bravely.

6. When the lieutenant will have finished his journey he will quickly return.

---

* See Note, p. 88.   † Indicative.   ‡ Rule 4, p. 39.

50 (A). Conjunctive Mood.

Present Tense.				Imperfect Tense.	
1. Poss-	im	5. Fĕr-	am	1. Poss-	em
2. Vĕl-	is		ās	2. Vell-	ēs
	ĭt		ăt	3. Noll-	ĕt
3. Nōl	īmŭs	6. Fī-	āmŭs	4. Mall-	ēmŭs
	ītĭs		ātĭs	5. Ferr-	
4. Māl	int	7. E-	ant	6. Fĭĕr-	ētĭs
				7. Ir-	ent

The Perfect-stem Tenses are formed regularly.

Imperative Mood.

Present.		Future.			
3. Nōl-ī*	nōl-ītĕ	Nōl-ītō	nōl-ītō	nōl-ītōtĕ	nōl-untō
5. Fĕr	fer-tĕ	Fer-tō	fer-tō	fĕr-tōtĕ	fĕr-untō
6. Fī	fī-tĕ				
7. I	ī-tĕ	I-tō	ī-tō	ī-tōtĕ	ĕ-untō

50 (B). Infinitive Mood.   Participles.

Presenč.	Perfect.	Future.	Present.	Future.
1. Possĕ	pŏtŭ-issĕ	———		———
2. Vellĕ	vŏlŭ-issĕ	———	Vŏl-ens	———
3. Nollĕ	nōlŭ-issĕ	———	Nōl-ens	———
4. Mallĕ	mālŭ-issĕ	———	Māl-ens	———
5. Ferrĕ	tŭl-issĕ	lāt-ūrŭs essĕ	Fĕr-ens	lāt-ūrŭs
6. Fĭĕrī	factŭs essĕ	factum īrī		
7. I-rĕ	īv-issĕ	ĭt-ūrŭs essĕ	I-ens (ĕunt-)	ĭt-ūrŭs

Fio has Part. Perf. Factŭs ; Gerundive, Făcĭendŭs.

Gerunds.   Supines.

2. Vŏl-end-	um			
3. Nōl-end-			———	
4. Māl-end-	ī		———	
5. Fĕr-end-	ō	5. Lăt-um	lāt-ū	
7. E-und-	ō	7. It-um	ĭt-ū	

8. The Passive of Fero is irregular in the following parts :—
Ind. Pres., Fĕrŏr, ferrĭs, fertŭr, fĕrĭmŭr, fĕrĭmĭnĭ, fĕruntur.
Conj. Imper., Fērr-ĕr, ferr-ērĭs, &c.
Imper. Pres., Ferrĕ, fĕrĭmĭnĭ. *Fut.*, fertŏr, fertŏr, fĕruntŏr.
Infin., Ferrĭ.

* Be thou unwilling, do not.

50 (C). 1. Si bonus esse velis, bonos ama.
2. Titus sine praesidio proficisci noluisset.
3. Pontem custodiemus, ne hostes fugere possint.
4. Fortius pugnavissent, si vincere voluissent.
5. Dux multa bella geret, ut consul fiat.*
6. Galli e finibus suis exire volebant.

1. Caesar was killed, that Rome might become free.*
2. The Gauls feared, lest the Romans should cross the river.
3. Give ye hostages, if ye are unwilling (subj.) to be killed.
4. The gates must be shut, lest the hostage may go out.
5. The famous leader was unwilling to be made consul.
6. Bear ye your burdens more patiently.

---

50 (D). 1. Nisi Romani fortissime pugnavissent, Britannos vincere non potuissent.
2. Britanni impetum equitatus nostri ferre non potuerunt.
3. Quum Britanni se defendere non poterant, legatos ad Caesarem miserunt.
4. Si ad te venire vellem, propter flumen non possem.
5. Noli fugere, si a duce laudari velis.
6. Si exire malis, tecum ibo.

1. They would have gone out from their borders, if Caesar had been willing.
2. The consul was exhorting the soldiers, that they might bear all dangers patiently.
3. Unless Caesar had crossed the river, he would not have been able to conquer Cassivelaunus.
4. When the Britons had fled, Caesar returned to the camp.
5. If the citizens had been unwilling to take arms, they would have been killed.
6. I should prefer to give wounds, (rather) than to receive (them).

---

* See Rule 4. p. 39.

51 (A). First Declension.

Fīlĭă, *a daughter*, and some others, have the Dat. and Abl. Pl. in -ābŭs, to distinguish them from Masculine Nouns of the Second Declension, as fīlĭābŭs.

Second Declension.

Fīlĭŭs, *a son*, gĕnĭŭs, *a familiar spirit*, and Proper Names in -ĭŭs, contract ĭĕ into ī in the Voc., as Fīlī, *O son*. The Genitive ĭī is often contracted into ĭ.

Dĕŭs, *a god*, has *Voc.* Dĕŭs, *Pl. Nom.* Dĕī or Dī, *Gen.* Dĕōrum or Dĕum, *Dat. and Abl.* Dĕīs or Dīs.

Third Declension.

Nāvĭs, turrĭs, and some others have *Acc.* -em or -im, *Abl.* -ĕ or -ī; Ignis has *Abl.* -ĕ or -ī.

Vīs (*f.* force, *Pl.* strength, *Acc.* vim, *Abl.* vī, *Pl.* vīr-es, -ĭum, -ĭbŭs), has no Gen. or Dat. Sing.

Prĕc -em (*f.* a prayer, *Dat.* prĕc -ī, *Abl.* prĕc -ĕ, *Plur.* prĕc -ēs, -um, -ĭbŭs) has no Nom. or Gen. Sing.

Op-em (*f.* help, *Pl.* riches, *Gen.* ŏp -ĭs, *Abl.* ŏp -ĕ, *Pl.* ŏp -ēs, -um, -ĭbŭs) has no Nom. or Dat. Sing.

Fourth Declension.

Portus and some others have -ŭbŭs or -ĭbŭs in the Dat. and Abl. Plur.

Dŏmŭs (*f.* a house) has *Sing. Dat.* -ŭī or -ō, *Abl.* -ŏ. *Plur. Acc.* -ūs or -ōs, *Gen.* -ŭum or ōrum.

---

51 (B). Compound Nouns.

The Republic.	An oath.	A matron.
N.V. Rēs-publĭcă, *f.*	Jus-jūrandum, *n.*	Māter-fămĭlĭas, *f*
Acc. Rem-publĭcam	Jus-jūrandum	Matrem-fămĭlĭas
Gen. Rĕī-publĭcae	Juris-jūrandī	Matrĭs-fămĭlĭas
Dat. Rĕī-publĭcae	Juri-jūrandō	Matrī-fămĭlĭas
Abl. Rĕ-publĭcā	Jure-jūrandō	Matrĕ-fămĭlĭas, &c

Learn and decline :—

Rhŏdănus, ī, *m.* the Rhone | Jūra, ae, *m.* the Jura
Rhēnus, i, *m.* the Rhine | Gāĭus, i, *m.* Gaius (as Filius)
Dĕa, ae, *f.* a goddess (as Filia) | Jūlĭus, i, *m.* Julius

Decline together :—

1. Flumen Rhodanus. 2. Mons Jura. 3. Gaius, vir fortis. 4. Gaius Julius Caesar. 5. Filia et filius. 6. Alta domus.

51 (C). *Rule* 10.—A Substantive agrees in Case with the word to which it is in Apposition, as

Nos *milites* Caesarem *ducem nostrum* laudamus.
We soldiers praise Caesar, our leader.

1. Rhodanus flumen longum et latum est.
2. Galli Romam, urbem pulcherrimam, ceperunt.
3. Moenia urbis Romae fortissima erant.
4. Romani montem Juram transibant.
5. Vos pueri flumen Rhenum non vidistis.
6. Caesar exercitum Galbae, viro forti, dat

1. We Britons never will be conquered.
2. The Gauls killed Titus, a very brave man.
3. The wars of Caesar, the Roman leader, were great.
4. My son, give thou this book to Titus, thy brother.
5. The town was surrounded by the river Rhone.
6. The fierce Cimbri were not able to conquer Gaius Julius Caesar.

_____

51 (D). 1. Titus, Caesaris legatus, in proelio interfectus est.
2. Rhodanus, flumen Galliae, velocissimus est.
3. Caesar copias Cassivelauni, ducis Britannorum, vicit.
4. Iter erat inter montem Juram et flumen Rhodanum.
5. Galba, rex potentissimus totius Galliae, fines latissimos habebat.
6. Dominus gladium Gaio, servo fideli, dederat.

1. Titus and Galba, very famous leaders, waged many wars.
2. The town was taken by the consul, a friend of Gaius Julius Caesar.
3. The Cimbri were unwilling to give their children (as) hostages.
4. The lieutenant will announce the victory to Titus, the son-in-law of my friend.
5. The names of Caesar and Titus, Roman citizens, will always be famous.
6. O Gaius Julius Caesar, thou conqueredst the Britons, thou wast not able to conquer thyself (tu-ipse).

52 (A). (1) Six Adjectives in -is form the Superlative by adding -lĭmŭs to the Stem ; as făcĭl-ĭs, făcil-lĭmŭs.

| Făcĭlĭs, *easy* | Sĭmĭlĭs, *like* | Grăcĭlĭs, *slender.* |
| Diffĭcĭlĭs, *difficult* | Dissĭmĭlĭs, *unlike* | Hŭmĭlĭs, *low.* |

(2) Adjectives in -dĭcŭs, -fĭcŭs, -vŏlŭs, add
Comp. -entĭŏr, *Sup.* -entissĭmŭs, to the Stem, as
magnĭfĭcŭs,* magnĭfĭcentĭŏr, magnĭfĭcentissĭmŭs.

(3) Adjectives in -us, pure (quus excepted), are com-pared with magis, *more;* maxime, *most,*† as
dŭbĭŭs, *doubtful;* măgĭs dŭbĭŭs, maxĭmē dŭbĭŭs.

---

52 (B). Learn and decline, with the English :—

Positive.	Comparative.	Superlative.
Bŏnŭs, *good*	mĕlĭŏr	optĭmŭs
Mălŭs, *bad*	pējŏr	pessĭmŭs
Magnŭs, *great*	mājŏr ‡	maxĭmŭs‡
Parvŭs, *small*	mĭnŏr ‖	mĭnĭmŭs‖
Multŭs, *much*	plūs §	plūrĭmŭs
Dīvĕs, *rich*	dītĭŏr	dītissĭmŭs
Extĕrŭs, *outside*	extĕrĭŏr	extrēmŭs or extĭmŭs
Infĕrŭs, *deep (below)*	infĕrĭŏr	infĭmŭs or īmŭs
Sŭpĕrŭs, *high (above)*	sŭpĕrĭŏr	suprēmŭs or summŭs
Postĕrŭs, *next (after)*	postĕrĭŏr	postrēmŭs or postŭmŭs

Some have no Positive, as

Comparative.	Superlative.
Intĕrĭŏr, *inner*	intĭmŭs, *inmost*
Prĭŏr, *former*	prīmŭs, *first*
Prŏpĭŏr, *nearer*	proxĭmŭs, *nearest, next*
Ultĕrĭŏr, *further*	ultĭmŭs, *furthest, last*
Cĭtĕrĭŏr, *hither*	cĭtĭmŭs, *hithermost*

---

* magnificent. † but pĭus, *dutiful*, makes pĭissĭmŭs.
‡ often used for elder, eldest. ‖ often for younger, youngest.
§ Sing. (Neut. only). plūr -ĭs, ĭ, ē ; Pl. plūr -ēs, ă ; -ĭum ; ĭbŭs

52 (C). *Rule* 11.—After a Comparative the Ablative answers the question, Than whom? Than what? as,

> Pax melior *bello* est.
> *Peace is better* than *war.*

1. Caesar major Tito erat.
2. Cives Romani ditissimi erant.
3. Plurimi hostium occisi sunt.
4. Hostes turrim humillimam fecerant.
5. Viri potentissimi non semper optimi sunt.
6. Minimae res maximae fiunt.

1. Who waged more wars than Caesar?
2. The Romans had very great forces in Gaul.
3. Caesar first conquered the Britons.
4. Britain is smaller than Gaul.
5. That victory was very doubtful.
6. These slaves were unwilling to bear heavier burdens.

---

52 (D). 1. Flumina Galliae majora sun` fluminibus Britanniae.
2. Caesar in Galliam citeriorem proficisci constituit.
3. In bello priore Romani victi erant.
4. Proximum iter in Galliam ulteriorem per montes erat.
5. Duo maxima bella a Caesare confecta erant.
6. Pessimi pueri meliores fieri possunt.

1. The Romans never had a greater leader than Caesar.
2. Very great cities were taken by the Romans.
3. A journey through the borders of the Senones was very difficult.
4. The smaller camp was pitched beneath the mountain.
5. The top* of the mountain was held by Titus.
6. The book, which I gave to thee, is very easy.

---

* Say, the highest (summus) mountain.

53 (A). 1. Sometimes the Subject or Object consists of a clause beginning with the word *that*, as—

	Subject.	Predicate.
(*a*)	*That* Caesar conquered the Gauls	is certain.

Subj.	Pred.	Object.
(*b*)	We know	*that* Caesar conquered the Gauls.

2. A Subject-clause or Object-clause is expressed in Latin by the Accusative and Infinitive, as

Caesarem (*Acc.*)   vicisse (*Infin.*)   Gallos.
That Caesar   *conquered* (Ind.) *the Gauls.*

Note (1) The word *that* is not translated into the Latin

(2) The Tense of the Infinitive in the Latin is the same as that of the Indicative in the English.

Rule 12.—Verbs of declaring, perceiving, knowing, thinking, and believing, often take after them an Object-clause.

---

53 (B). 1. Learn and conjugate :—

1. **Spēr-o**, -āre, -āvi, -ātum, I hope.
2. **Dīc-o**, -ĕre, dix-i, dict-um, I say, tell.
3. **Crēd-o**, -ĕre, -ĭdi, -ĭtum, I believe, trust, entrust.
4. **Cognosc-o**, -ĕre, cognōv-i, cognĭt-um, I ascertain, perceive.
5. **Sc-ĭo**, -īre, īvi or ĭi, ītum, I know.
6. **Pollĭc-ĕor**, -ēri, ĭtus, *dep.* I promise (voluntarily).

2. Give all their 3rd Persons—(1) Singular, and (2) Plural, with the English.

3. Say the Infinitive (Active and Passive) of any Verbs in B 24—2 *l.*

53 (C). 1. Audio Caesarem milites laudare.

2. Scimus Gallos Romam cepisse.

3. Spero nostros milites victuros esse.

4. Servus nuntiat portas fractas esse.

5. Caesar cognovit montem ab hostibus teneri.

6. Galba dicit rem esse facillimam.

1. I know that the soldiers love Caesar.

2. We have heard that the Romans conquered Britain.

3. Titus promises that he will come quickly.

4. The citizens say that the city is (being) attacked.

5. They do not believe that the town has been taken.

6. We know that good boys are happy.

---

53 (D). 1. Caesari nuntiant hostes flumen transire.

2. Quis non credit Romam a Gallis captam esse?

3. Scimus Romanos castra vallo fossaque munivisse.

4. Omnes sperant hostes victum iri.

5. Britanni polliciti sunt se Caesari obsides daturos (esse).*

6. Cimbri dixerunt se obsides accipere, non dare.

1. I do not believe that Caesar quickly conquered the Britons.

2. We know that the Romans have very good leaders.

3. The lieutenant announces to Caesar that the harbour is defended with ships.

4. Titus ascertained that the town was surrounded by a broad river.

5. The consul says that the city will be fortified with ramparts.

6. Caesar heard that great forces of the enemy had been drawn up.

---

* Note.—Esse is often omitted from the Inf. Fut.

54 (A). 1. Participles are Verbal Adjectives, and agree with their Substantives in Gender, Number, and Case.

2. In English the Participle Perfect usually stands *after* its Noun, with the sign *being* or *having been*, as

Galli	victi	fugerunt.
The Gauls	*being* or *having been* } *conquered*	*fled.*

3. When the Participle Perfect is translated *before* its Noun, the sign *being* or *having been* is omitted, as

Caesar	sequitur	Gallos victos.
Caesar	*pursues*	*the conquered Gauls.*

4. Repeat all the Participles, Active and Passive, of the four Conjugations, and of the Deponent Verb Hortor, giving the English.

---

54 (B). 1. Which Participles are formed with the Present (or Clipt) Stem? Which with the Supine Stem?

2. Distinguish between the Signs of the Participle Perfect of a Passive and a Deponent Verb.

3. Form the Participles of any Verbs on pp. 44, 45, and of the Deponent Verbs on p. 83, and give the English of them.

Rule 13.—Participles govern the same Cases as their Verbs.

54 (C). 1. Titus fortissime pugnans occiditur.
2. Hostem fugientem sequitur.
3. Galli Romam, urbem munitam, ceperunt.
4. Signifer vulneratus fugere nolebat.
5. Miles obsidem telum tenentem occidit.
6. Dicunt servum per apertam portam fugisse.

1. We saw the slave bearing a burden.
2. Cassivelaunus, being conquered by Caesar, fled.
3. Many soldiers, having followed the army, were killed.
4. The Gauls, being frightened at* our approach, took up arms.
5. Caesar heard that the Britons had very great forces drawn up.   [the river.
6. The enemy, endeavouring to flee, are hindered by

---

54 (D). 1. Dux, milites hortatus, signum pugnae dat.
2. Titus missus cum equitatu ad castra venit.
3. Cum legionibus tribus e castris profectus ad oppidum venit.
4. Cives, veriti ne occiderentur, fugere conabantur.
5. Caesari ab urbe proficiscenti victoria nuntiata est.
6. Hi pueri laudandi sunt, illi puniendi.

1. The soldier, being wounded by a dart, was not able to fight.
2. Titus having feared lest the enemy might attack the camp, sends a lieutenant to† Caesar.
3. The leader of the conquered Gauls killed himself.
4. The cruel slave wounded the head of the horse with a broken dart.
5. The Gauls, having attacked the army too eagerly, were killed.
6. Galba says that the gates are to be defended.‡

---

* Say, by.   † ad.   ‡ Say, meet to be defended.

55 (A). 1. An independent clause, consisting of a Noun and a Participle in the Ablative Case, is used to name the Time or Occasion, *When.*

This clause is called in Latin the Ablative Abso-lute, and answers to the Nominative* Absolute in English, as

Urbe	captā (Abl. Abs.)	cives fugerunt.
The city	*being taken (Nom. Abs.)*	*the citizens fled.*

2. The Ablative Absolute may often be translated by other forms, as

Urbe capta, *when* the city *was* taken.

---

55 (B). 3. When a Noun or Adjective is used instead of the Participle in the Absolute Clause, the word *being* must be placed before it in the English, as

Caesare	consule.
Caesar	being *consul.*

4. Words used to enlarge the Absolute Clause com-monly stand between the Noun and the Participle, as,

Urbe *a Caesare* captā.
The city having been taken by Caesar.

Rule 14.—The Ablative names the Time or Occa-sion, *When.*

---

* *i.e.,* it is without the *Sign* of the Ablative.

55 (C). 1. Oppido capto, praesidium interficiunt.
2. Legatis missis, Britanni obsides dederunt.
3. Equo vulnerato, consul fugere non poterat.
4. Caesar, obsidibus acceptis, in Senones proficiscitur.
5. Duce hortante, milites acriter pugnant.
6. Navibus fractis, Romani in Galliam redire non poterant.

1. A signal being given, the Gauls attack the town.
2. The darts having been thrown, they fight with swords.
3. The camp being pitched, they prepare to make an attack.
4. The fields having been laid waste, he leads the army into the borders of Cassivelaunus.
5. The thing being ascertained, they determine to cross the river.
6. Peace being made, the lieutenants return to* Caesar.

---

55 (D). 1. Acie duplici instructa, ad castra venerunt.
2. Gravibus acceptis vulneribus, Romani iter facere non poterant.
3. Cognito Caesaris adventu, hostes se defendere parant.
4. Vastatis omnibus eorum agris, legiones in castra redibunt.
5. Castris ante oppidum positis, portas claudi jubet.
6. Duce absente, legatus pugnare timebat.

1. These things having been ascertained, Caesar orders Titus to set out with three legions.
2. Arms and hostages having been received, Titus will make peace with them.
3. The consul ordering (it), the citizens prepare to fortify the citadel.
4. A great part of our army being killed, the Gauls hope that they will conquer.
5. Two very great wars being finished, Caesar sets out for† hither Gaul.
6. Thou being (our) leader, O Caesar, we shall never be conquered.

---

* ad.   † Say, into

Say what Part of Speech the word is, and if

1. **A Substantive.**—Nom. and Gen. Sing.? Declension? Gender? Number? and Case? Governed by?* Why?

2. **An Adjective.**—Nom. Sing.? Degree?† Like? Gender? Number? and Case? Agreeing with? Why?

3. **A Verb** (Finite).—Principal Parts? Conjugation? Voice? Mood? Tense? Number? and Person? To agree with its Subject? Why?

(Infinitive).—Principal Parts? Conjugation? Voice? Mood? Tense? Rule?

(Participle).—Principal Parts? What Participle? Gender? Number? and Case? Agreeing with? Why?

4. **A Pronoun.**—What kind? and if—

(a) Personal or Reflexive.—Nom. and Gen. Sing.? Gender? Number? and Case? Why?

(b) Adjective.—From? Gender? Number? and Case? Agreeing with? Why?

(c) Relative.—From? Gender? Number? Agreeing with its Antecedent? Case? Why?

5. **An Adverb.**—Degree (if any)? Qualifying?

6. **A Preposition.**—Governing?

7. **A Conjunction.**—What kind?

---

* If Nominative, omit this.   † If Positive, this may be omitted.

VOCABULARY.—LATIN WORDS.

LIST OF ABBREVIATIONS.

abl.	=	ablative.	*n.*	=	neuter.
acc.	=	accusative.	*num.*	=	numeral.
adj.	=	adjective.	*p.*	=	page.
adv.	=	adverb.	*P.*	=	plural only.
anom.	=	anomalous.	*pers.*	=	pers.
c.	=	common gender.	*poss.*	=	possessive.
comp.	=	comparative.	*prep.*	=	preposition.
conj.	=	conjunction.	*pron.*	=	pronoun, pronominal.
dem.	=	demonstrative.	*rel.*	=	relative.
dep.	=	deponent.	*S.*	=	singular only.
f.	=	feminine.	*subs.*	=	substantive.
interrog.	=	interrogative.	*sup.*	=	superlative.
m.	=	masculine.	*v.*	=	verb.

1, 2, 3, 4, indicate the conjugation of a verb.

A.

ă, ăb, *prep.* with *abl.*, by, from.

absens, entis, *adj.*, absent.

accĭpĭo, cēpi, ceptum, 3, I receive.

ăcĕr, cris, cre, *adj.*, sharp, eager.

ăcĭes, ēi, *f.*, an army in line of battle.

ăd, *prep.* with *acc.*, to, for.

ădŏrĭor, ortus, 4, *dep.*, I attack (suddenly).

adventus, ūs, *m. S.*, an approach.

aeger, gra, grum, *adj.*, sick.

ăger, gri, *m.*, a field.

agmĕn, ĭnis, *n.*, an army on the march.

ălĭus, a, ud, *pron. adj.*, other, another.

alter, tĕra, tĕrum, *pron. adj.*, the one, the other.

altus, a, um, *adj.*, high, deep.

ămant, (they) love.

ămăt, (he, she, it) loves.

ambō, bae, bo, both (together).

ămīcus, i, *m.*, a friend.

ămo, āvi, ātum, 1, I love.

ănĭmăl, ālis, *n.*, an animal.

antĕ, *prep.* with *acc.*, before.

ăpĕrĭo, ĕrŭi, ertum, 4, I open, disclose.

arbĭter, tri, *m.*, a judge, umpire.

armă, ōrum, *n. P.*, arms.

arx, arcis, *f.*, a citadel.

asper, ĕra, ĕrum, *adj.*, rough, fierce.
audĭo, īvi, ītum, 4, I hear.

B.

bellum, i, *n.*, war.
bŏnus, a, um, *adj.*, good.
brĕvis, e, *adj.*, short.
Brĭtanni, ōrum, *m. P.*, the Britons.
Brĭtannĭa, ae, *f. S.*, Britain.

C.

Caesar, ăris, *m. S.*, Caesar.
Cantĭum, i, *n. S.*, Kent.
căpĭo, cēpi, captum, 3, I take, capture.
căpŭt, ĭtis, *n.*, a head, source.
carrus, i, *m.*, a waggon.
căsa, ae, *f.*, a cottage.
Cassĭvĕlaunus, i, *m. S.*, Cassivelaunus.
castră, ōrum, *n. P.*, a camp.
cĕler, ĕris, ĕre, *adj.*, swift.
Cimbri, ōrum, *m. P.*, the Cimbri.
cingo, nxi, nctum, 3. I surround.
circum, *prep.* with *acc.*, around.
cĭtĕrĭor, us, *adj.*, hither.
cĭvis, is, *c.*, a citizen.
clārus, a, um, *adj.*, bright, famous.
claudo, si, sum, 3, I shut, close.
cognosco, nōvi, nĭtum, 3, I ascertain, perceive.
concĭlĭum, i, *n.*, a council.
confĭcĭo, fēci, fectum, 3, I finish.
cōnor, ātus, 1, *dep.*, I endeavour, attempt.
constĭtŭo, ŭi, ūtum, 3, I determine, appoint.
consul, ŭlis, *m.*, a consul.
contră, *prep.* with *acc.*, against.

cōpĭae, ārum, *f. P.*, forces.
cornu, ūs, *n.*, horn, wing of an army.
corpus, oris, *n.*, a body.
crēber, bra, brum, *adj.*, frequent.
crēdĭt, (he, she, it) entrusts.
crēdo, dĭdi, dĭtum, 3, I believe, trust, entrust.
crēdunt, (they) entrust.
crūdēlis, e, *adj.*, cruel.
cum, *prep.* with *abl.*, with, together with.
currus, ūs, *m.*, a chariot.
custōdĭo, īvi, ītum, 4, I guard.

D.

dant, (they) give.
dăt, (he, she, it) gives.
dē, *prep.* with *abl.*, from, concerning.
dĕa, ae, *f.*, a goddess (p. 101).
dēfendĭt, (he, she, it) defends.
dēfendo, di, sum, 3, I defend.
dēfendunt, (they) defend.
dens, ntis, *m.*, a tooth.
dĕus, i, *m.*, a god (p. 101).
dextĕr, tĕra, tĕrum, or tra, trum, *adj.*, right.
dīco, dixi, dictum, 3, I say.
dĭes, ĕi, *c.* in sing., *m.* in plu., a day.
diffĭcĭlis, e, *adj.*, difficult.
dissĭmĭlis, e, *adj.*, unlike.
dīvĕs, ĭtis, *adj.*, rich.
do, dăre, dĕdi, dătum, 1, I give.
dŏcent, (they) teach.
dŏcĕo, cŭi, ctum, 2, I teach.
dŏcĕt, (he, she, it) teaches.
dŏmĭnus, i, *m.*, a lord.
dŏmus, ūs, *f.*, a house (p. 101)
dŭbĭus, a, um, *adj.*, doubtful.

I

dūco, duxi, ductum, 3, I lead, draw.

dŭŏ, ae. ŏ, *num. adj.*, two.

duplex, ĭcis, *adj.*, double.

dūrus, a, um, *adj.*, hard, cruel.

dux, dŭcis, *c.*, a leader.

E.

ē, *prep.* (see *ex*).

ĕgo, mĕi, *pers. pron.*, I (p. 85).

ĕo, īre, īvi or ĭi, ĭtum, *anom. v.* I go (p. 97).

ĕquĭtātus, ūs, *m. S.*, cavalry.

ĕquus, i, *m.*, a horse.

ĕt, *conj.*, and.

ex, or ē. *prep.* with *abl.*, out of, from.

exĕo, īre, ivi (or ĭi), ĭtum, *anom. v.* I go out (p. 97).

exercĭtus, ūs, *m.*, an army.

extĕrus, a, um, *adj.*, outward.

extrā, *prep.* with *acc.*, outside.

F.

făber, bri, *m.*, workman.

făcĭlis, e, *adj.*, easy.

făcĭo, fēci, factum, 3, I make, do.

făcĭt, (he, she, it) makes.

făcĭunt, (they) make.

fēlix, ĭcis, *adj.*, happy, successful.

fĕrax, ācis, *adj.*, fruitful.

fĕro, ferre, tŭli, lātum, *anom. v.* I bear, endure (p. 97).

fĕrox, ōcis, *adj.*, fierce.

fĭdēlis, e, *adj.*, faithful.

fĭdes, ĕi, *f. S.*, faith.

fīlĭa, ae, *f.*, a daughter (p. 101).

fīlĭus, i, *m.*, a son (p. 101).

fīnes, ĭum, *m. P.*, borders.

fīnio, īvi, ĭtum, 4, I finish, end.

fĭo, fĭĕri, factus, *anom. v.*, I become, am made, or done.

firmus, a, um, *adj.*, firm, strong.

flūmen, ĭnis, *n.*, a river.

fortĭor, us, *adj.*, stronger.

fortis, e, *adj.*, strong, brave.

fossa, ae, *f.*, a ditch, trench.

frangĭt, (he, she, it) breaks.

frango, frēgi, fractum, 3, I break.

frangunt, (they) break.

frāter, tris, *m.*, a brother.

fŭgĭo, fŭgi, fŭgĭtum, 3, I flee, fly.

fūnis is, *m.*, a rope.

G.

Gaius, i, *m. S.*, Gaius.

Galba, ae, *m. S.*, Galba.

Gallĭa, ae, *f. S.*, Gaul (France).

Gallus, i, *m.*, a Gaul.

gĕner, ĕri, *m.*, a son-in-law.

gĕnu, ūs, *n.*, the knee.

gĕro, gessi, gestum, 3, I carry on, wage.

glădĭus, i, *m.*, a sword.

grăcĭlis, e, *adj.*, slender.

grădus, ūs, *m.*, a step.

grăvĭor, us, *adj.*, heavier.

grăvis, e, *adj.*, heavy, severe.

H.

hăbent, (they) have.

hăbĕo, ŭi, ĭtum, 2, I have.

hăbĕt, (he, she, it) has.

hĭc, haec, hōc, *dem. pron.*, this.

hortor, ātus, 1, *dep.*, I exhort

hostis, is, *c.*, an enemy.

hŭmĭlis, e, *adj.*, low.

I.

ictus, ūs, *m.*, a blow.
īdem, ĕădem, ĭdem, *dem. pron.*, the same (p. 87).
ignis, is, *m.*, fire.
illĕ, illă, illŭd, *dem. pron.*, he, she, it, that (p. 87).
impĕdĭo, īvi, ītum, 4, I hinder.
impĕdĭt, (he, she, it) hinders.
impĕdĭunt, (they) hinder.
impĕtus, ūs, *m.*, an attack.
in, *prep.* with *abl.*, in, upon, among ; with *acc.*, into, against.
infĕrus, a, um, *adj.*, deep, (below).
ingens, entis, *adj.*, immense.
innŏcens, entis, *adj.*, innocent.
instrŭo, xi, ctum, 3, I draw up.
intĕr, *prep.* with *acc.*, between, among.
interfĭcĭo, fēci, fectum, 3, I kill, slay.
intĕrĭor, us, *adj. comp.*, inner.
intrā, *prep.* with *acc.*, within.
ipsĕ, a um, *pron.*, myself, thyself, etc. (p. 87).
is, ĕa, ĭd, *dem. pron.*, he, she, it, that (p. 87).
istĕ, a, ud, *dem. pron.*, that (near you), (p. 87).
ĭtĕr, ĭtĭnĕris, *n.*, a journey, march, road.

J.

jăcĭo, jēci, jactum, 3, I throw, cast.
jam, *adv.*, now, already.
jŭbĕo, jussi, jussum, 2, I order, command.
Jūlĭus, i, *m. S.*, Julius.
Jūra, ae, *m. S.*, the Jura, a mountain-chain between the Rhine and the Rhone
jusjūrandum, jūrisjūrandi, *n.*, an oath.

L.

lăpis, ĭdis, *m*, a stone.
lātus, a, um, *adj.*, broad, wide.
laudant, (they) praise.
laudăt, (he, she, it) praises.
laudo, āvi, ātum, 1, I praise.
lēgātus, i, *m.*, a lieutenant, ambassador.
lĕgĭo, ōnis, *f.*, a legion.
lĕvis, e, *adj.*, light.
līber, ĕra, ĕrum, *adj.*, free.
līber, bri, *m.*, a book.
lībĕri, ōrum, *m. P.*, children.
longus, a, um, *adj*, long.

M.

măgister, tri, *m.*, a master.
magnĭfĭcus, a, um, *adj.*, magnificent.
magnus, a, um, *adj.*, great.
mălo, malle, mālŭi, *anom. v.*, I prefer (p. 97).
mălus, a, um, *adj.*, bad.
mănus, ūs, *f.*, a hand.
măre, is, *n.*, the sea.
māterfămĭlĭas, mātrisfămĭlĭas, *f.*, a matron.
mĕlĭor, us, better, *comp.* of bonus.
mensa, ae, *f.*, a table.
mĕrīdĭes, ēi, *m. S.*, noon.
mĕus, a, um, *poss. pron.*, my, mine.
mīles, ĭtis, *m.*, a soldier.
mīror, ātus, 1, *dep.*, I wonder at, admire.
mĭser, ĕra, ĕrum, *adj.*, wretched.
mitto, mīsi, missum, 3, I send, throw.

moenĭa, ĭum, *n. P.*, ramparts.
mŏnĕo, ŭi, ĭtum, 2, I advise.
mons, ntis, *m.*, a mountain.
multus, a, um, *adj.*, much, many.
mūnĭo, īvi, ītum, 4, I fortify.
mūrus, i, *m.*, a wall.

N.

nauta, ae, *m.*, a sailor.
nāvis, is, *f.*, a ship.
nē, *conj.*, lest, that not.
neuter, tra, trum, *adj.*, neither.
nĭger, gra, grum, *adj.*, black.
nĭsĭ, *conj.*, unless.
nōlo, nōlŭi, *anom. v.*, I am unwilling (p. 97).
nōmen, ĭnis, *n.*, a name.
nōn, *adv.*, not.
noster, tra, trum, *poss. pron.*, our, ours.
nullus, a, um, *adj.*, no, none (p. 91).
nunquam, *adv.*, never.
nuntĭo, āvi, ātum, 1, I announce.

O.

obses, ĭdis, *c.*, a hostage.
occĭdit, (he, she, it) kills.
occĭdo, ĭdi, īsum, 3, I kill, slay.
occĭdunt, (they) kill.
omnis, e, *adj.*, every, all.
ŏnus, ĕris, *n.*, a burden.
ŏpem, is, *f.*, help (see p. 101).
oppĭdum, i, *n.*, a town.
oppugno, āvi, ātum, 1, I attack, assault.
ŏvis, is, *f.*, a sheep.

P.

păro, āvi, ātum, 1, I prepare.
pars, partis, *f.*, part.
parvus, a, um, *adj.*, little, small.
pătĭens, entis, *adj.*, patient.

pax, pācis, *f. S.*, peace.
pĕr, *prep.* with *acc.*, through.
pĕrīcŭlum, i, *n.*, danger.
pernĭcĭes, ēi, *f. S.*, destruction.
pĭus, a, um, *adj.*, dutiful.
plānĭtĭes, ēi, *f. S.*, a plain.
plēbes, ēi, *f. S.*, the common people.
plūrĭmus, a, um, *sup.* of multus.
plus, *comp.* of multus (p. 103).
pollĭcĕor, ĭtus, 2, *dep.*, I promise.
pōno, pŏsŭi, pŏsĭtum, 3, I place, pitch.
pons, ntis, *m.*, a bridge.
porta, ae, *f.*, a gate.
porto, āvi, ātum, 1, I carry.
portus, ūs, *m.*, a harbour.
possum, pŏtŭi, *anom. v.*, I can, am able (p. 97).
post, *prep.* with *acc.*, after, behind.
postĕrus, a, um, *adj.*, next (after).
pŏtens, entis, *adj.*, powerful.
praebĕo, ŭi, ĭtum, 2, I afford, supply.
praesĭdĭum, i, *n.*, a garrison, guard.
prĕcem, is, *f.*, prayer (p. 101).
prīmus, *sup.* of prior (p. 103).
prĭor, prĭus, ōris, *comp. adj.*, former.
prŏ, *prep.* with *abl.*, before, for, instead of.
proelĭum, i, *n.*, an engagement, battle.
prŏfĭcĭscor, fectus, 3, *dep.*, I set out, advance.
prŏpĭor, us, *adj.*, nearer.
propter, *prep.* with *acc.*, on account of.
proxĭmus, *sup.* of propior.

prūdens, entis, *adj.*, prudent.
pŭer, ĕri, *m.*, a boy.
pugna, ae, *f.*, a battle.
pugno, āvi, ātum, 1, I fight.
pulcher, chra, chrum, *adj.*, beautiful, fair.
pūnĭo, īvi, ītum, 4, I punish.

Q.

quam, *conj.*, than.
quĕ, *conj.*, and (p. 95).
qui, quae, quod, *rel. pron.*, who, which, what.
quis (quis), quid, *interrog. pron.*, who? what?
quis, qua, quid, *indef. pron.*, any, any one.
quum, *conj.*, when

R.

rĕcens, entis, *adj.*, fresh, recent.
rĕdĕo, īvi or ĭi, ĭtum, *anom. v.*, I return (p. 97).
regnum, i, *n.*, a kingdom.
rĕgo, rexi, rectum, 3, I rule.
rēs, ĕi, *f.*, a thing, affair.
rēspublĭca, rēipublĭcae, *f.*, the Republic.
rētĕ, is, *n.*, a net.
rex, rēgis, *m.*, a king.
Rhēnus, i, *m. S.*, the Rhine.
Rhŏdănus, i, *m. S.*, the Rhone.
Rōma, ae, *f. S.*, Rome.
Rōmānus, a, um, *adj.*, Roman.

S.

săcer, cra, crum, *adj.*, sacred.
săgitta, ae, *f.*, an arrow.
scĭo, īvi, ītum 4, I know.
scūtum, i, *n.*, a shield.
sĕ (sese), sŭi, *pers. pron.*, himself, etc. (p. 85).
sĕd, *conj.*, but.

sempĕr, *adv.*, always.
sĕnātus, ūs, *m. S.*, the Senate.
Sĕnŏnes, um, *m. P.*, the Senones. [follow.
sĕquor, sĕcūtus, 3, *dep.*, I
servus, i, *m.*, a slave.
sĭ, *conj.*, if. [bearer.
signĭfer, eri, *m.*, a standard-
signum, i, *n.*, standard, sign.
sĭmĭlis, e, *adj.*, like.
sĭnĕ, *prep.* with *abl.*, without.
sŏcer, eri, *m.*, a father-in-law.
sōlus, a, um, *adj.*, only, alone.
sŏror, ōris, *f.*, a sister.
spĕcĭes, ēi, *f.*, an appearance.
spēro, āvi, ātum, 1, I hope.
spēs, spĕi, *f.*, hope.
sŭb, *prep.* with *acc.* and *abl.*, under, beneath, below.
sŭpĕrus, a, um, *adj.*, high, (above).
sŭus, a, um, *poss. pron.*, his, her, its, their.

T.

tēlum, i, *n.*, a dart.
tĕnent, (they) hold.
tĕnĕo, ŭi, tentum, 2, I hold.
tĕner, ĕra, ĕrum, *adj.*, tender.
tĕnĕt, (he, she, it) holds.
terrent, (they) frighten.
terrĕo, ŭi, ĭtum, 2, I frighten.
terrĕt, (he, she, it) frightens.
tĭment, (they) fear.
tĭmĕo, ŭi, —, 2, I fear.
tĭmĕt, (he, she, it) fears.
tĭmĭdus, a, um, *adj.*, timid.
Tĭtus, i, *m. S.*, Titus.
tōtus, a, um, *adj.*, the whole.
trans, *prep.* with *acc.*, across.
transĕo, ĭi, ĭtum, *anom. v.*, I cross over (p. 97).
trēs, trĭa, *num. adj.*, three.

tristis, e, *adj.*, sad.
tū, tŭi, *pers. pron.*, thou (p. 85).
turris, is, *f.*, a tower.
tŭus, a, um, *poss. pron.*, thy, thine.

U.

ullus, a, um, *adj.*, any.
ultĕrĭor, us, *adj.*, latter.
ultĭmus, a, um, *adj.*, last.
unquam, *adv.*, ever.
ūnus, a, um, *num. adj.*, one, alone.
urbs, urbis, *f.*, the city.
ŭt, *conj.*, in order that, that.
ŭter, tra, trum, *pron. adj.*, which (of the two)?
ŭterquĕ, trăquĕ, trumquĕ, *pron. adj.*, each.

V.

vallum, i, *n.*, a mound (with palisades).
vastant, (they) lay-waste.
vastăt, (he, she, it) lays-waste.
vasto, āvi, ātum, 1, I lay-waste.

vēlox, ōcis, *adj.*, swift.
vĕnĭo, vēni, ventum, 4, I come.
vĕrĕor, ĭtus, 2, *dep.*, I fear.
vester, tra, trum, *poss. pron.*, your, yours.
victōrĭa, ae, *f.*, victory
vīcus, i, *m.*, a village.
vĭdent, (they) see.
vĭdĕo, vīdi, vīsum, 2, I see.
vĭdĕt, (he, she, it) sees.
vincĭt, (he, she, it) conquers.
vinco, vīci, victum, 3, I conquer.
vincunt, (they) conquer.
vĭr, vĭri, *m.*, a man.
vis, *f.*, force (p. 101).
vīta, ae, *f.*, life.
vŏlo, velle, vŏlŭi, *anom. v.*, I wish, am willing (p. 97).
vox, vōcis, *f. S.*, a voice.
vulnĕrant, (they) wound.
vulnĕrăt, (he, she, it) wounds.
vulnĕro, āvi, ātum, 1, I wound.
vulnus, ĕris, *n.*, a wound.

VOCABULARY—ENGLISH WORDS.

A.
able (am), possum, pŏtŭi, *anom. v.* (p. 97).
absent, absens, entis, *adj.*
across, trans, *prep.* with *acc.*
admire, mīror, ātus, 1, *dep.*
advance, prŏfĭciscor, fectus, 3, *dep.*
advise, mŏnĕo, ŭi, ĭtum, 2.
affair, rēs, ĕi, *f.*
afford, praebĕo, ŭi, ĭtum, 2.
after, post, *prep.* with *acc.*
against, contrā, in, *prep.* with *acc.*
all, omnis, e, *adj.*
alone, sōlus, a, um ; ūnus, a, um, *adj.*
already, jam, *adv.*
always, sempĕr, *adv.*
ambassador, lēgātus, i, *m.*
among, intĕr, in, *prep.* with *acc.*
and, ĕt, *conj.*
animal, ănĭmăl, ālis, *n.*
announce, nuntĭo, āvi, ātum, 1.
another, ălĭus, ă, ŭd, *pron. adj.*
any, ullus, a, um, *pron. adj.*
appearance, spĕcĭes, ĕi, *f.*
appoint, constĭtŭo, ŭi, ūtum, 3.
approach, adventus, ūs, *m. S.*
arms, armă, ōrum, *n. P.*
army, exercĭtus, ūs, *m.*

army (in line of battle), ăcĭes, ēi, *f.* [ĭnis, *n.*
army (on the march), agmĕn,
around, circum, *prep.* with *acc.*
arrow, săgitta, ae, *f.*
ascertain, cognosco, nōvi, nĭtum, 3.
assault, oppugno, āvi, ātum, 1.
attack, impĕtus, ūs, *m.*
attack (to), oppugno āvi, ātum, 1.
attack (suddenly), ădŏrĭor, ortus, 4, *dep.*
attempt, cōnor, ātus, 1, *dep.*

B.
bad, mălus, a, ŭm, *adj.*
battle, pugna, ae, *f.;* proelĭum, i, *n.*
bear, fĕro, tŭli, lātum, *anom. v.* (p. 97).
beautiful, pulcher, chra, chrum, *adj.*
become, fīo, factus, *anom. v.* (p. 97).
before, antĕ, *prep.* with *acc.;* prō, *prep.* with *abl.*
behind, post, *prep.* with *acc.*
believe, crēdo, dĭdi, dĭtum, 3.
beneath, sŭb, *prep.* with *acc.* and *abl.*

better, mĕlĭor, us, *adj.*
between, intĕr, *prep.* with *acc.*
black, nĭger, gra, grum, *adj.*
blow, ictus, ūs, *m.*
body, corpus, ŏris, *n.*
book, lĭber, bri, *m.*
borders, fīnes, ĭum, *m. P.*
both, ŭterquĕ, ambō (p. 91).
boy, pŭer, ĕri, *m.*
brave, fortis, e, *adj.*
break (they), frangunt.
break (to), frango, frēgi, fractum, 3.
breaks (he), frangĭt.
bridge, pons, tis, *m.*
Britain, Brĭtannĭa, ae, *f. S.*
Britons, Brĭtanni, ōrum, *m. P.*
broad, lātus, a, um, *adj.*
brother, frāter, tris, *m.*
burden, ŏnus, ĕris, *n.*
but, sĕd, *conj.*
by, ă, ăb, *prep.* with *abl.*

C.

Caesar, Caesar, ăris, *m. S.*
camp, castră, ōrum, *n. P.*
can, possum, pŏtŭi, *anom. v.* (*p.* 97).
capture, căpĭo, cēpi, captum, 3.
carry, porto, āvi, ātum, 1.
carry on (war), gĕro, gessi, gestum, 3.　　　　[i, *m. S.*
Cassivelaunus, Cassĭvĕlaunus,
cast, jăcĭo, jēci, jactum, 3.
cavalry, ĕquĭtātus, ūs, *m. S.*
chariot, currus, ūs, *m.*
children, lĭbĕri, ōrum, *m. P.*
Cimbri, Cimbri, ōrum, *m. P.*
citadel, arx, arcis, *f.*
citizen, cīvis, is, *c.*
city, urbs, urbis, *f.*
close, claudo, si, sum, 3.
come, vĕnĭo, vēni, ventum, 4.

command, jŭbeo, jussi, jussum, 2.
common people, plēbes, ēi, *f. S.*
concerning, dē, *prep.* with *abl.*
conquer (they), vincunt.
conquer (to), vinco, vīci, victum, 3.
conquers, vincĭt.
consul, consŭl, ŭlis, *m.*
cottage, căsa, ae, *f.*
council, concĭlĭum, i, *n.*
cross over, transĕo, ĭi, ĭtum (p. 97).
cruel, crūdēlis, e; dūrus, a, um, *adj.*

D.

danger, pĕrīcŭlum, i, *n.*
dart, tēlum, i, *n.*
daughter, fīlĭa, ae, *f.* (p. 101).
day, dĭes, ēi, *c.* in *Sing.,* *m.* in *Plu.*
deep, altus, a, um, *adj.*
defend (they), dēfendunt.
defend (to), dēfendo, di, sum, 3.
defends (he), dēfendĭt.
destruction, pernĭcĭēs, ēi, *f. S.*
determine, constĭtŭo, ŭi, ūtum, 3.
difficult, diffĭcĭlis, e, *adj.*
disclose, ăpĕrĭo, ĕrŭi, ertum, 4.
ditch, fossa, ae, *f.*
do, făcĭo, fēci, factum, 3.
done (to be), fīo, factus, *anom. v.* (p. 97).
double, duplex, ĭcis, *adj.*
doubtful, dŭbĭus, a, um, *adj.*
draw, dūco, duxi, ductum, 3.
draw up, instrŭo, xi, ctum, 3.

E.

each, ŭterquĕ (p. 91).
eager, ācer, cris, cre, *adj.*
easy, făcĭlis, e, *adj.*

end, fīnĭo, īvi, ītum, 4.
endeavour, cōnor, ātus, 1, *dep.*
endure, fĕro, tŭli, lātum, *anom.*
   v. (p. 97).
enemy, hostis, is, *c.*
engagement, proelĭum, i, *n.*
entrust (they), crēdunt.
entrust (to), crēdo, dĭdi,
   dĭtum, 3.
entrusts, crēdit.
ever, unquam, *adv.*
every, omnis, e, *adj.*
exhort, hortor, ātus, 1, *dep.*

F.

fair, pulcher, chra, chrum, *adj.*
faith, fīdes, ĕi, *f. S.*
faithful, fĭdēlis, e, *adj.*
famous, clārus, a, um, *adj.*
father-in-law, sŏcer, ĕri, *m.*
fear (they), tĭment.
fear (to), tĭmĕo, ŭi, —, 2 ;
   vĕrĕor, ĭtus, 2, *dep.*
fears (he), tĭmet.
field, ăger, gri, *m.*
fierce, aspĕr, ĕra, ĕrum ; fĕrox,
   ōcis, *adj.*
fight, pugno, āvi, ātum, 1.
finish, fīnĭo, īvi, ītum, 4 ; confĭcĭo, fēci, fectum, 3.
fire, ignis, is, *m.*
firm, firmus, a, um, *adj.*
flee, }
fly, } fŭgĭo, fūgi, fŭgĭtum, 3.
follow, sĕquor, sĕcūtus, 3.
for, prō, *prep.* with *abl.*
force, vīs, *f.* (p. 101).
forces, cōpĭae, ārum, *f. P.*
former, prĭor, us, *adj.*
fortify, mūnĭo, īvi, ītum, 4.
free, līber, ĕra, ĕrum, *adj.*
frequent, crēber, bra, brum, *adj.*
friend, ămīcus, i, *m.*

frighten (they), terrent.
frighten (to), terrĕo, ŭi, ĭtum, 2.
frightens (he), terret.
from, ā (ăb), dē, ē (ex), *prep.*
   with *abl.*
fruitful, fĕrax, ācis, *adj.*
further, ultĕrĭor, us, *adj.*

G.

Gaius, Gaius, i, *m. S.*
Galba, ae, *m. S.*
garrison, praesĭdĭum, i, *n.*
gate, porta, ae, *f.*
Gaul, Gallĭa, ae, *f. S.*
Gaul, (a), Gallus, i, *m.*
give (they), dant.
give (to), do, dĕdi, dătum, 1.
gives (he), dăt.
go, ĕo, īvi (or ĭi), ĭtum, *anom.*
   v. (p. 97).
go out, exĕo, īvi, (or ĭi), ĭtum,
   anom. v. (p. 97).
god, dĕus, i, *m.* (p. 101).
goddess, dĕa, ae, *f.* (p. 101).
good, bŏnus, a, um, *adj.*
great, magnus, a, um, *adj.*
guard (subs.), praesĭdĭum, ĭ, *n.*
guard (to), custōdĭo, īvi, ītum,
   4.

H.

hand, mănus, ūs, *f.*
happy, fēlix, īcis, *adj.*
harbour, portus, ūs, *m.*
hard, dūrus, a, um, *adj.*
has (he), hăbĕt.
have (they), hăbent.
have (to), hăbĕo, ŭi, ĭtum, 2.
head, căput, ĭtis, *n.*
heavier, grăvĭor, us, *adj.*
heavy, grăvis, e, *adj.*
he, ĭs, ĕa, ĭd, *dem. pron.* (p. 87)
hear, audĭo, īvi, ītum, 4.
help, opem, is, *f.* (p. 101).

her, sŭus, a, um, *poss. pron.*
herself, sē (sese), sŭi (p. 85).
high, altus, a, um, *adj.*
himself, sē (sese) sŭi (p. 85).
hinder (they), impĕdĭunt.
hinder (to), impĕdĭo, īvi, ītum, 4.
hinders (he), impĕdĭt.
hither, cĭtĕrĭor, us, *adj.*
his, sŭus, a, um, *poss. pron.*
hold (they), tĕnent.
hold (to), tĕnĕo, tĕnŭi, tentum, 4.
holds (he), tĕnĕt.
hope, spēs, ēi, *f. subs*
hope (to), spēro, āvi, ātum, I.
horn, cornū, ūs, *n.*
horse, ĕquus, i, *m.*
hostage, obses, ĭdis, *c.*
house, dŏmus, ūs, *f.* (p. 101).

I.

I, ĕgo, mĕi, *pers. pron.* (p. 85).
if, sī, *conj.*
immense, ingens, entis, *adj.*
in, in, *prep.* with *acc.*
inner, intĕrĭor, us, *adj.*
innocent, innŏcens, entis, *adj.*
instead of, prō, *prep.* with *abl.*
into, in, *prep.* with *acc.*
it, ĭs. ĕa, ĭd, *dem. pron.* (p. 87).
its, sŭus. a, um, *pron.* (p. 85).
itself, sē (sese), sŭi, *pron.* (p. 87).

J.

journey, ĭter, ĭtĭnĕris, *n.*
judge, arbĭter, tri, *m.*
Julius, Jūlĭus, i, *m. S.*
Jura, Jūra, ae, *m. S.*

K.

Kent, Cantĭum, i, *n. S.*
kill (they), occīdunt.

kill (to), occīdo, īdi, īsum, 3;
    interfīcĭo, fēci, fectum, 3.
kills (he), occīdĭt.
king, rex, rēgis, *m.*
kingdom, regnum, i, *n.*
knee, gĕnu, ūs, *n.*
know, scĭo, īvi, ītum, 4.

L.

lay-waste (they), vastant.
lay-waste (to), vasto, āvi, ātum, I.
lays-waste (he), vastăt.
lead, dūco, duxi, ductum, 3.
leader, dux, dŭcis, *c.*
legion, lĕgĭo, ōnis, *f.*
lest, nē, *conj.*
lieutenant, lēgātus, i, *m.*
life, vīta, ae, *f.*
light, lĕvis, e, *adj.*
like, sĭmĭlis, e, *adj.*
little, parvus, ă, um, *adj.*
long, longus, a, um, *adj.*
lord, dŏmĭnus, i, *m.*
love (they), ămant.
love (to), ămo, āvi, ātum, I.
loves (he), ămăt.
lowly, hŭmĭlis, e, *adj.*

M.

made (am), fīo, factus, *anom. v.* (p. 97).
magnificent, magnĭfĭcus, a, um, *adj.*
make (they), făcĭunt.
make (to), făcĭo, fēci, factum, 3.
makes (he), făcĭt.
man, vĭr, vĭri, *m.*
many, multus, a, um, *adj.*
march, ĭter, ĭtĭnĕris, *n.*
master, măgister, tri, *m.*
matron, măter-fămĭlias, mātris-fămĭlias, *f.*

mine, měus, a, um, *poss. pron.*
mound, vallum, i, *n.*
mountain, mons, montis, *m.*
much, multus, a, um, *adj.*
my, měus, a, um, *poss. pron.*
myself, ěgo-ipse.

N.

name, nōmen, ĭnis, *n.*
nearer, prŏpĭor, us, *adj.*
neither, neuter, tra, trum, *pron. adj.*
net, rētě, is, *n.*
never, nunquam, *adv.*
next, proxĭmus, a, um, *adj.*
no, nullus, a, um, *pron. adj.*
none, nullus, a, um, *pron. adj.*
noon, měrĭdĭes, ēi, *m. S.*
not, nōn, *adv.*
now, jām, *adv.*

O.

oath, jus-jūrandum, jūris-jū-randi, *n.*
on account of, propter, *prep.* with *acc.*
one, ūnus, a, um, *num. adj.* (p. 91).
one (the), alter, ěra, ěrum, *pron. adj.* (p. 91).
open, ăpěrĭo, ěrŭi, ertum, 4.
opposite to, contrā, *prep.* with *acc.*
order, jŭběo, jussi, jussum, 2.
other, ălĭus, a, ŭd, *pron. adj.* (p. 91).
other (the), alter, ěra, ěrum, *pron. adj.* (p. 91).
our, ours, noster, tra, trum, *poss. pron.*
out of, ex, ē, *prep.* with *abl.*
outside, extrā, *prep.* with *acc.*
outward, extěrus, a, um, *adj.*

P.

part, pars, partis, *f.*
patient, pătĭens, entis, *adj.*
peace, pax, pācis, *f. S.*
people, plēbes, ēi, *f. S.*
perceive, cognosco, nōvi, nĭ-tum, 3.
pious, pĭus, a, ᴜm, *adj.*
pitch, pōno, pŏsŭi, posĭtum, 3.
place, pōno, pŏsŭi, pŏsĭtum, 3.
plain, plānĭties, ēi, *f. S.*
powerful, pŏtens, entis, *adj.*
praise (they), laudant.
praise (to), laudo, āvi, ātum, 1.
praises (he), laudăt.
prayer, prěcem, is, *f.* (p. 101)
prefer, mālo, ŭi, *anom. v.* (p. 97).
prepare, păro, āvi, ātum, 1.
promise, pollĭcěor, ĭcĭtus, 2, *dep.*
prudent, prūdens, entis, *adj.*
punish, pūnĭo, īvi, ītum, 4.
pursue, sěquor, sěcūtus, 3, *dep.*

Q.

quick, cělěr, ěris, ěre, *adj.*

R.

ramparts, moenĭa, ĭum, *n. P.*
receive, accĭpĭo, cēpi, ceptum, 3.
recent, rěcens, entis, *adj.*
republic, rēs-publĭca, rěī-pub-licae, *f. S.*
return, rěděo, īvi, ītum, *anom. v.* (p. 97).
Rhine, Rhēnus, i, *m. S.*
Rhone, Rhŏdănus, i, *m. S.*
rich, dīves, ĭtis, *adj.*
riches, ŏpes, um, *f.* (p. 101).
right, dexter, tra, trum, *adj.*
river, flūmen, ĭnis, *n.*

road, ĭter, ĭtĭneris, *n.*
Rome, Rōma, ae, *f. S.*
Roman, Rōmānus, a, um, *adj.*
rope, fūnis, is, *m.*
rough, asper, ĕra, ĕrum, *adj.*
rule, rĕgo, rexi, rectum, 3.

S.

sacred, săcer, cra, crum, *adj.*
sad, tristis, ĕ, *adj.*
sailor, nauta, ae, *m.*
same, ĭdem, ĕădem, ĭdem, *dem. pron.* (p. 87).
say, dīco, dixi, dictum, 3.
sea, mărĕ, is, *n.*
see (they), vĭdent.
see (to), vĭdĕo, vīdi, vīsum, 2.
sees (he), vĭdĕt.
self, ipsĕ, a, um, *pron. adj.* (p. 91).
senate, sĕnātus, ūs, *m. S.*
send, mitto, mīsi, missum, 3.
Senones, Sĕnŏnes, um, *m. P.*
set out, prŏfĭciscor, fectus, 3, *dep.*
severe, grăvis, e, *adj.*
sharp, ācer, cris, cre, *adj.*
she, ĕă : *see* ĭs (p. 87).
sheep, ŏvis, is, *f.*
shield, scūtum, i, *n.*
ship, nāvis, is, *f.*
short, brĕvis, ĕ, *adj.*
shut, claudo, si, sum, 3.
sick, aeger, gră, grum, *adj.*
signal, signum, i, *n.*
sister, sŏrŏr, ōris, *f.*
slave, servus, i, *m.*
slay, occīdo, īdi, īsum, 3.
slender, grăcĭlis, ĕ, *adj.*
small, parvŭs, a, um, *adj.*
soldier, mīles, ĭtis, *m.*
some, ălĭus, a, ŭd, *pron. adj.*
son, fīlĭus, i, *m.* (p. 101).
son-in-law, gĕner, ĕri, *m.*

source, căput, ĭtis, *n.*
standard, signum, *n.*
standard-bearer, signĭfer, ĕri, *m.*
step, grădus, ūs, *m.*
stone, lăpis, ĭdis, *m.*
strength, vīs, *f.* (p. 101).
strong, firmus, a, um ; fortis, e, *adj.*
stronger, fortĭor, ŭs, *adj.*
successful, felix. *adj.*
supply, praebĕo, uı, ītum, 2.
surround, cingo, cinxi, cinctum, 3.
swift, cĕler, ĕris, ĕre ; vēlox, ōcis, *adj.*
sword, glădĭus, i, *m*

T.

table, mensa, ae, *f.*
take, căpĭo, cēpi, captum, 3.
teach (they), dŏcent.
teach (to), dŏcĕo, ŭi, tum, 2.
teaches (he), dŏcĕt.
tell, dīco, dixi, dictum, 3.
tender, tĕner, a, um, *adj.*
than, quam, *conj.*
that (conj.), ŭt.
that (pron.), illĕ, ă, ŭd (p. 87).
their, sŭus, a, um, *poss. pron.*
themselves, sē (sese), sŭi, *pron.* (p. 85).
they, ĭs, ĕa, ĭd, *dem. pron.* (p. 87).
thine, tŭus, a, um, *poss. pron.*
thing, rēs, rēi, *f.*
this, hīc, haec, hōc, *dem. pron.* (p. 87).
thou, tu, tŭi, *pers. pron.* (p. 85).
three, trēs, trĭă, *num. adj.* (p. 91).
through, pĕr, *prep.* with *acc.*
throw, jăcĭo, jēci, jactum, 3 ; mitto, mīsi, missum, 3.

thy, tŭus, a, um, *poss. pron.*
thyself, tu, tŭi, *pers. pron.*
(p. 85).
timid, tĭmĭdus, a, um, *adj.*
Titus, Tītus, i, *m. S.*
to, ăd, *prep.* with *acc.*
tooth, dens, dentis, *m.*
tower, turris, is, *f.*
town, oppĭdum, i, *n.*
trust, crēdo, dĭdi, dĭtum, 3.
two, dŭŏ, dŭae, dŭŏ, *num. adj.*
(p. 91).

U.

umpire, arbĭter, tri, *m.*
under, sŭb, *prep.* with *acc.* and
abl.
unless, nĭsĭ, *conj.*
unlike, dissĭmĭlis, ĕ, *adj.*
unwilling, nōlo, ŭi, *anom. v.*
(p. 97).
upon, in, *prep.* with *ace.*

V.

victory, victōrĭa, ae, *f.*
village, vīcus, i, *m.*
voice, vox, vōcis, *f.*

W.

wage, gĕro, gessi, gestum, 3.
waggon, carrus, i, *m.*
wall, mūrus, i, *m.*

war, bellum, i, *n.*
weapon, tēlum, i, *n.*
what, quĭd (p. 89).
when, quum, *conj.*
who, ⎰ quī, quae, quŏd, *rel.*
which, ⎱ *pron.*; quĭs (quis),
      ⎱ quĭd, *interrog. pron.*
which (of two), ŭter, tra, trum,
pron, adj.
whole, tōtus, a, um, *adj.* (p.
91).
wide, lātus, ă, um, *adj.*
willing (am), vŏlo, ŭi, *anom.*
v. (p. 97).
wing, cornu, ūs, *n.*
wish, vŏlo, ŭi, *anom. v.* (p. 97).
with, cum, *prep.* with *abl.*
within, intrā, *prep.* with *acc.*
without, sĭnĕ, *prep.* with *abl.*
wonder at, mīror, ātus, 1, *dep.*
workman, făber, bri, *m.*
wound (a), vulnus, ĕris, *n.*
wound (they), vulnĕrant.
wound (to), vulnĕro, āvi, ātum,
1.
wounds (he), vulnĕrăt.
wretched, mĭser, ĕra, ĕrum,
adj.

Y.

your, yours, vester, tră, trum,
poss. pron.

FINIS.

Spottiswoode & Co. Ltd., Printers, Colchester, London and Eton.

GREEK LESSONS;

SHEWING HOW USEFUL AND HOW EASY IT IS FOR EVERY ONE TO LEARN GREEK. ·

By W. H. MORRIS.

PART I. price 2s. 6d.; PART II. price 1s.; COMPLETE, price 3s. KEY to PART I. price 2s.

Extract from the Preface:—

What is the use of Greek ?

It has three very important uses.

First. There are so many words in English (and new ones are daily being introduced) derived from Greek, that some knowledge of the Greek language is an essential of a sound English education ; and it is, besides, of the greatest use in learning Latin and modern languages.

Second. 'There never was such a language to *educate the mind* of man.' It is 'the most subtle and powerful language that ever flowed from the tongue of man;' and yet it is 'an easy language.'*

Third. Above all, it is the language in which, *before all others*, God chose to reveal His will to us—the language of the New Testament. 'No other language will ever express the meaning of God's Spirit as it may be seen to be expressed and known by those who read the New Testament in its original Greek. In this the English tongue *totally fails*.'*

Thus to the every-day man, to the scholar, and especially to the Christian, Greek is of practical value.

---

* 'The Intelligent Study of Scripture.' By Dean Alford.

Lightning Source UK Ltd.
Milton Keynes UK
UKHW012026301118
333277UK00004B/106/P